INSTANT POT
COOKBOOK

100 Traditional Recipes from Around the World

(Chinese, Thai, Italian, Mexican, and Brazilian)

Introduction

I want to thank you and congratulate you for choosing this book, *"Instant Pot Cookbook: 100 Traditional Recipes from Around the World (Chinese, Thai, Italian, Mexican and Brazilian)."*

One thing is true: the Instant Pot is a revolutionary kitchen appliance. If you have it, or planning to have it, based on the great feedback on how great it is, you can bet that you will not be disappointed. There might be one challenge though; although the Instant Pot has many functions and can cook almost anything, the notion of cooking 'everything and anything' can be overwhelming. What exactly can you cook? How does it work? What does the many settings mean to you as a user? How do you take care of the Instant Pot, And how exactly should you choose the right Instant Pot if you are in the process of buying one?

Well, to make your choice of the Instant Pot as seamless as possible and to maximize your user experience, this book will answer these and many other questions that you might have about the Instant Pot. In addition, as you will realize, having a wide array of recipes to start with is definitely a worthwhile investment.

This book has all that for you and many more. It contains 100 delicious finger-licking recipes that will not only transform your cooking to exclusively use the Instant Pot,but also revolutionize your palate in ways you've never thought. You will discover ways to prepare Chinese, Thai, Italian, Brazilian, as well as Mexican dishes with the Instant Pot to take your cooking to the next level.

If you love cooking and love tasty food, this book is for you.

Thanks again for choosing this book. I hope you enjoy it!

Contents

Introduction 3

Must Knows Before Buying An Instant Pot 9

Basic Abbreviations And Terms 9
Functionality Basics 11

Common Mishaps and How to Avoid Them 15

Different Parts and Designs of Instant Pots 19

Different Parts of Instant Pots 29
Tips & Tricks to Keep In Mind When Working With Instant
Pots 39

How to Convert Normal Recipes into Instant Pot
Recipes 40

Why You MUST own an Instant Pot 44

Breakfast Recipes 47

Rice Pudding... 47
Instant Pot Steel Cut Oats 49
Chinese Rice Porridge 52
Apple Bread with Caramel Topping 54
Vanilla Steel Cut Oats 56
Hard Boiled Eggs... 58
Almond Steel Cut Oats 59
Instant Pot Egg Cupcakes...61
Pumpkin Porridge 63
Crustless Tomato Spinach Quiche 64

Lunch Recipes 66

Italian Sausage and Peppers 66
Beef Ribs with Thai Sauce 68
Sweet Potato and Red Curry Soup 70
Thai Chicken and Eggplant 72

Chicken Cordon Bleu Casserole 74

Italian Pulled Pork... 76

Mexican Chicken Soup 78

Vegetable Beef Stew 80

Pressure Cooked Pot Roast 82

Pasta with Lentil Bolognese 84

Instant Pot Pasta Florentine 86

Chicken Tortilla Soup.. 88

Tiger Prawn Risotto... 90

Broccoli Rabe and Chickpeas 92

Instant Pot Brazilian Potato Salad 94

Instant Pot Brazilian Chicken Soup 96

Vegan Feijoada 98

Mexican Rice 100

Cabbage Roll Soup... 102

Lasagna Soup.. 104

Cream Cheese Chicken Chilli 106

Hamburger Soup 108

No Noodle Lasagne 110

Mexican Rice 112

Multigrain Rice... 114

Sweet Potato with Italian Turkey Sausage........................... 115

Dal Makhani 117

Instant Pot Saag.. 119

Chicken Congee 121

Instant Pot Congee 122

Instant Pot Veggie Stew..124

Carne Guisada 127

Green Bean Casserole..129

Instant Pot Cauliflower and Sweet Potato 131

Veggie Soup 133

Dinner Recipes 135

Mexican Polenta 135

Instant Pot Chile Verde 137

Mexican Casserole..138

Instant Pot Pork and Hominy stew 140
Instant Pot Mexican Rice 142
Instant Pot Braised Beef.. 144
Rice with Sausage 146
Instant Pot Beef and Broccoli Stir-fry 148
Instant Pot Egg and Pork Congee 150
Thai Curry...152
Instant Pot Fish Chowder..154
Pork and Potatoes...156
Instant Pot Penne and Meatballs 158
Instant Pot Chicken 160
Chicken Carbonara 162
Brazilian Bean and Meat Stew 164
Instant Pot Macaroni and Cheese 166
Chinese Beef Stew... 168
Instant Pot Oat Rice with Sausage 170
Pork Stew with Vegetables 172
Instant Pot Acini Di Pepe Beef Soup..............................174
Chicken Marsala 176
Instant Pot Picadillo 178
Instant Pot Keema 180
Instant Pot Vegetable Pulao 182
Curried Potatoes 184
Pasta Fagioli... 186
Instant Pot Soup 188
Chicken Chili.. 190
Instant Pot Italian Chicken 192
Thai Peanut Chicken.. 194
Instant Pot Cranberry beans 196
Chili Macaroni 198
Chinese Congee..200
Azuki Bean Soup..202
Steamed Corns..204
Thai Carrot Soup 205
Instant Pot Popcorn..207

Instant Pot Potato Salad...208
Instant Pot Lemon Cheesecake 210
Instant Pot Chocolate Cake 212
Lemon Curd...214
Tapioca Pudding..216
Caramel Pot de Creme...218
Dulce de Leche... 220
Egg Muffins 222
Mexican-Inspired Corn On The Cob 224
Instant Pot Magic Cake 226
Instant Pot Applesauce... 228
Beef Barley Soup.. 230
Steamed Crab Legs 233
Instant Pot Tomato Soup 234
Chocolate Cheesecake 236
Bread Pudding... 237
Instant Pot Pumpkin Pie 239

Conclusion... **241**

If you haven't bought an Instant Pot yet, you need to begin the process by critically considering some things before you make the decision. This will ensure that your purchase is based on knowledge and not on unfounded assumptions. This also applies to anyone who purchased the Instant Pot recently without understanding it properly. That's where we will begin...

Must Knows Before Buying An Instant Pot

Before buying an instant pot, or Instapot, you need to know a few things first because, like everything else in life, things are bound to get a bit tricky if you don't understand the Instant Pot properly. Let's start with the definition to ensure you understand what we are talking about.

An instant pot is simply an amazing multipurpose pressure cooker, which operates like a pressure cooker, yogurt maker, rice cooker and many other functions- except you get tastier results!

I know you might be wondering when you are ever going to get the hang of it so that you can start gobbling up your instant pot made meals. To make you start well, here are a few essentials to keep at the back of your mind before getting yourself one of these magic machines:

Basic Abbreviations And Terms

As you are already aware, the Instant Pot is really a pressure cooker. The process of using it calls for use of certain strategies which you need to understand if you are to have a smooth time while using it. Let's discuss some of these terms, which you will find in many Instant Pot recipes.

QPR (Quick Pressure Release)

This is a common term that you will see in recipes and manuals. This just means that you manually release the pressure quickly by twisting the vent valve positioned at the very top of the lid to 'open'.

When to use it: the unwritten rule is to use quick release for veggies (unless you are cooking baby mush food), non-foaming foods and if your Instant Pot isn't filled to the maximum. You can also use it to add ingredients as you cook, for instance veggies (for beef stew) and then proceed with your cooking until done.

How to do it: use a towel to cover the vent to diffuse anything that might come out like the strong pressure of steam. Slowly turn the valve then close it quickly if you notice food sputtering. Open it slowly, a little at a time until the force reduces- make sure to be smart about it and be cautious. At first, you might feel a bit nervous to handle the valve so you can use tongs instead.

NPR (Natural Pressure Release)

This means that you let the Instant Pot naturally release pressure. You just have to leave the vent valve alone until it releases all pressure by its own. You will know it has when you see the silver button on top of the lid go down. In most cases, this setting is used for meat- well, unless you like dry leathered jerky for dinner, foaming starchy foods and a pot filled up to the max line.

For instance, if a recipe calls for '10 NPR', this means that you have to wait until when the panel reads 'L0:10' to open the vent to manually release the pressure. Don't forget to start slow as you release the pressure.

PIP (Pot in Pot)

This means the use of another container inside your pot. During pressure cooking (up to 248F), the Instant Pot does not get as hot as an oven as you bake so you can use glass, stainless steel, silicone cups or any other oven proof container to place inside your instant pot.

With that understanding, let's now discuss some other basics of the Instant Pot.

Functionality Basics

The great thing about an Instant Pot is that it is precisely designed with buttons for specific functions that will help cook your food better. The sensors associated with the buttons know exactly how hot a specific food should be and will help to prevent the food from overcooking or burning- but you still control the time, so don't leave it all to the Pot.

Some of the wonderful cooking and safety features that you need to understand to make cooking with the pot easy for you include the following:

Keep Warm/Cancel

This cancels any program that has been previously set hence putting the cooker in standby. When the cooker is in this standby mode, pressing this key will set forth the keep warm program, which can last to about 100 hours.

Soup

This setting is used to make a variety of broths and soups. The default is set at 30 minutes of high pressure although this can be adjusted using the ADJUST or plus and minus buttons.

Porridge

This is for making oatmeal or porridge of various grains. The default here is high pressure for 20 minutes. Make sure you DON'T use quick release for this setting as it will result in a major mess.

Note: Only use this setting with the pressure valve set to SEALING.

Poultry

As the name suggests, this setting is used to make meals with poultry and the default is set at high pressure for 15 minutes.

Meat/Stew

This setting is used for making meats or stew and the default is set at high pressure for 35 minutes. You can add time by selecting 'MORE' if you want that bone stripping effect on your meat.

Bean/Chili

This setting is specifically meant for making chili or cooking beans. The default is high pressure for 30 minutes but if you want well done beans, then select 'MORE'.

Rice

This is the setting which turns your Instant Pot into a rice cooker. It's an amazing program for cooking either parboiled or regular rice. For the best experience, make sure to use the provided water measurements inside the pot and the rice measuring cup that comes with the pot. The default for this setting is automatic and cooks rice at low pressure.

For instance, the manual indicates that the cooking duration for the rice changes automatically depending on the food content. Cooking 2 cups of rice will take approximately 12 minutes pressure keeping time and more cups will take more time accordingly.

When working pressure is reached, the pressure keeping time will be shown but the total cooking time is not displayed. On this setting, the 'ADJUST' key has no effect whatsoever.

Multigrain

This setting is used to cook a mixture of grains such as brown rice, mung beans, wild rice etc. The set default for this setting is 40 minutes of high pressure while the 'LESS' setting is 20 minutes of cooking time while the 'MORE' setting involves 45 minutes of just warm water soaking which is followed by 60 minutes of cooking time on high pressure.

Steam

This setting is used for steaming seafood, veggies or reheating foods. You should not NPR on this setting as you will be likely to overcook your food. The default here is 10 minutes of high pressure cooking. You will require about 1 to 2 cups for steaming and make sure you use a basket or a steamer rack as this setting can burn food which is in direct contact with the pot.

Manual

This button allows you to manually set your own pressure and cooking time (the maximum time is 240 minutes). This button is best used when you have a recipe indicating that you should cook on high pressure for a specified number of minutes.

Sauté

This setting is for open lid browning, sautéing or simmering.

For regular browning: 'Normal'- 160 degrees C (320 degrees F)

For darker browning: 'More'- 170 degrees C (338 degrees F)

For light browning: 'Less'- 105 degrees C (221 degrees F)

Slow Cook

This setting converts your Instant Pot into a slow cooker, which can run to up to 40 hours- but the default is Normal heat for 4 hours of cook time.

Yogurt

There are 3 programs on this setting: make yogurt, making Jiu Niang (fermented rice) and pasteurizing milk. The default of this setting is 8 hours of incubation. To pasteurize milk, adjust to 'More' and to ferment rice or proof bread, adjust to 'Less'.

Timer (For delayed cooking)

Usually, many people confuse this setting with an actual cooking timer, which crushes their expectations on the cooker.

To use this setting the right way:

Start off by selecting your cooking program (e.g. 'Steam' or any other function except the 'Yogurt' and 'Sauté') and then press on the timer button. Use the '+' and '-' for setting the delayed hours. Press on the timer setting again to change the minutes.

The time that you have set is the delayed time before the program begins. This is where you can set the pot to start cooking a few hours before you get home or wake up so that you find freshly cooked dinner, lunch or breakfast. You should allow for both sufficient cooking time and cooking down time before serving.

With that understanding of the basics i.e. an understanding of the functions and abbreviations, we will now move on to getting rid of any confusion that you might have while using the Instant Pot and how to avoid it.

Common Mishaps and How to Avoid Them

Making mistakes is perfectly normal. But when you know the mistakes in advance, the chances of making them becomes less, which can save you a great deal of negative consequences. Some of the common mistakes that people make when using the Instant Pot include the following:

Overfilling the Instant Pot

Most new users overfill their Instapot with liquid or food way up to the Max Line (the point where the contents of the Instapot should not exceed) or even past the Max Line. This is dangerous as it can risk clogging of the Venting knob.

Therefore, always be mindful and aware that the Max Line on the Instant Pot is **not** meant for pressure cooking. For pressure cooking, the maximum is two thirds full and for foods that expand during cooking (like dried veggies and grains) the maximum is ½ full for pressure cooking.

But if you overfill the pot, don't worry. Just make sure you use NPR to stay clean and safe.

Forgetting to place back the inner pot before adding the ingredients

As silly as this might sound (how can you forget to put back the inner pot?), this mistake happens more than often. This can wreak havoc in the kitchen and lead to immature damage to your new cooking tool.

To avoid this, every time you remove the inner pot, for whatever reason, place wooden spoon, silicone mat or a glass lid on top of the Instapot so that you can remember to put it back when you see the mark.

Forgetting to completely turn the Venting knob to the "Sealing" position

As mentioned earlier, it can be a bit confusing to use the instant pot in the beginning, which leaves room for many users to forget to turn the Instant Pot's venting knob to the "Sealing" position while cooking.

Here is a great tip to make sure you don't forget: Every time you start pressure cooking, always make sure that the venting knob is on the "Sealing" position. Do not walk away until you make sure that the Floating Valve has actually started popping up.

Using QR for foamy foods or when the Instapot is overfilled

When you are a new Instant Pot user, you might be still unsure of when to use the NPR or QPR. The chances of splattering are very high when you use the wrong kind of release i.e. using quick release when cooking foamy foods like beans.

Just make sure you use NPR for such foods- as mentioned before. But some foamy foods call for QR, like most pasta recipes. If you come across such, release the pressure gradually. Turn the knob a little at a time.

Using the timer button to set cooking time

As I said earlier, the Timer button is for delayed cooking. When you want to start cooking, check if the 'Timer' button is lit (you will see a green light). If it is, press the Keep Warm/Cancel button to start again.

Cooking liquid

The amount of liquid required for cooking can be really tricky for a new user. You can either make the mistake of having too little liquid (too thick) or too much liquid (runny).

If there is not enough water for cooking or the liquid is too thick, then the instant pot cannot be able to produce enough steam to get up to pressure. Unless it is stated differently in a recipe:

- It is recommended that new users should use 1 cup of pure liquid until comfortable enough with the gadget.

- After the pressure cooking cycle, always add a thickener such as arrowroot, cornstarch, and flour or potato starch.

On the other hand, if the cooking liquid is in excess in the Instapot, the overall cooking time will be increased (both getting up to pressure time and Natural Release time). This can lead to your food overcooking. Besides, too much liquid will dilute your seasoning leading to a flavorless dish. Unless it is stated differently in a recipe, use 1 cup of total liquid until completely comfortable with the gadget.

Using hot liquid in dishes that require cold liquid

If you are running into problems where almost all of your Instapot meals are undercooked, then this might be the problem. Using hot liquid to cook a meal that calls for cold liquid reduces the time for coming up to pressure.

The food might come out undercooked since food initially starts to cook once the Instapot is heating up and coming to pressure and this time is shortened by hot water.

Always use cold liquid to cook or you can adjust the cooking time required in the recipe accordingly.

Putting the Instant Pot on the stovetop and turning the dial

Due to limited counter space or pure convenience, you may find yourself placing your instant pot on the stovetop. One thing may lead to another and you might find your beauty having a burnt bottom.

It's as simple as this; just don't put your Instapot directly on the stovetop. If you have to do it, then lay a wooden board in between the pot and the stovetop to prevent unseen disasters.

Using the rice setting for cooking any kind of rice

There have been common complaints about the Instapot and cooking rice but don't be discouraged just yet. Different types of rice require different cooking times and water so completely depending on the Default setting is not really a good idea.

For the perfect results, use the 'Manual' button to get ultimate control on your cooking time and method.

Let's take the discussion a little further where we will discuss the different parts and designs of the Instant Pot so that you understand how to choose one like a pro and how to use yours even if you are a complete beginner.

Different Parts and Designs of Instant Pots

Different Designs of Instant Pots

I have to be honest here- the Instant Pot names sound like chemical reactions- so let's go ahead and break down the best Instapot designs!

Instant Pot IP-DUO60 7-in-1 Programmable Pressure Cooker

Price range: $132.45

This is a large pressure cooker with all the whistles and bells. It features the following functions: rice cooker, steamer, sauté/browning, pressure cooking, yogurt maker and warmer.

The instant pot is equipped with a user friendly control panel with 14 smart programs which are effortless to use. The pot has a bottom that is stainless steel (with a stainless steam rack and handle) that ensures that food is cooked evenly and thoroughly.

The pros:

- Has a user friendly control panel

- Has multiple cooking functions

- Contains a steam rack that is made of stainless steel

The cons:

- It has a small interior volume

- The gasket is prone to retaining odors

- It can burn thinner liquids and sauces

Instant Pot IP-LUX50 6-in-1 Programmable Pressure Cooker, 5Qt/900W

Price range: $113.16

This is a 5 quart pressure cooker that is large enough to serve a gathering. It comes in 2 models:

A 6-in-1 programmable pressure cooker- which is also a rice cooker, warmer, slow cooker, steamer and can brown and sauté food

A 7-in-1 programmable pressure cooker- which can perform all the above functions and adds in a yogurt making option.

This instant pot design also contains 10 in built smart programs inclusive of soup, steam, meat/stew, chili, multigrain and slow cook.

The pros:

- It is available in either 6-in-1 or 7-in-1 unit (you make the choice)

- Contains 10 built-in programs

- It has a large capacity

The cons:

- There is insufficient setup/cooking manual instructions

- The tempered glass lid is excluded

- Sometimes the preset programs aren't correct

Instant Pot IP-LUX60 6-in-1 Programmable Pressure Cooker, 6-Quart 1000-Watt

Price range: $111.58

This instant pot is popular for its ability to cook food faster while at the same time conserving energy. And don't be fooled by its fast cook time as this pot also reserves nutrients and flavors giving delectable results.

This gadget is a slow cooker, steamer, pressure cooker, rice cooker and can brown and sauté food.

The cooker also has a durable stainless steel cooking bottom that enables even heat distribution. You can manually set the pot to up to 120 minutes of cook time or delay cook time for up to 24 hours.

The pot comes with a stainless steel steam rack, rice paddle, soup soon, recipes, instructions, measuring cup and cook time tables.

The Pros:

- Reduced energy consumption as it is fast
- Has speedy cook times
- Includes delayed cook time

The Cons:

- The gasket tends to retain food aroma

- The instruction booklet can do better

- You need to carefully place the valve needs for sealing or venting

Instant Pot IP-Smart Bluetooth-Enabled Multifunctional Pressure Cooker

Price range: $229.95

This model features handy Bluetooth technology that lets you program and monitor the pot from your tablet or smart phone. As a bonus, the pot is also way faster with reduced energy consumption.

Just like other Instapot units, it is multi-functional and can be used as a slow cooker, yogurt maker, food warmer, steamer, pressure cooker, rice cooker, porridge maker, sauté pan and much more.

It has a free app known as Instant Pot Smart Cooker that is compatible with Android, iPad and iPhone, which allows easy and total control of your meals. The highlights include multi-functional cooking and 14 built in smart programs.

The Pros:

- It comes with a free app

- It is Bluetooth smart and compatible with Android, iPad and iPhone

- Contains 14 built-in smart programs

The Cons:

- Some people complain of weak Bluetooth signal making it less 'easy'

- The recipes included could be better

- Sometimes pairing can be tricky

Instant Pot IP-DUO50 7-in-1 Programmable Pressure Cooker with Stainless Steel Cooking Pot and Exterior, 5Qt/900W

Price range: $126.95

This is a multifunctional Instapot that works as a rice cooker, steamer, food warmer, pressure cooker, yogurt maker, slow cooker, porridge maker and browns and sautés food. It is equipped with lots of safety mechanisms.

The slow cooker includes delayed cooking for up to 24 hours together with manual and automatic keep warm settings. A manual pressure setting features up to 120 minutes of cook time and you can select times between 30 minutes and 20 hours for all your recipes.

Most of the functions include 3 adjustable modes which gives you easier control over your dishes.

For making yogurt, the pot can hold up to 5 liters of milk at a time.

The Pros:

- The pot features Keep-warm settings

- It can hold up to 5 liters of milk at a time when you want to make yogurt

- It also features functions with adjustable modes

The cons:

- The preparation times can be a bit slow

- The pot takes time to build the required amount of pressure

- It has an initial learning curve and may take a while to get used to

All the Instant Pots above are almost identical in their respective parts. In the next part, we will discuss some of the components of the Instant Pot.

Different Parts of Instant Pots

Base unit

This is the outer body of the Instant Pot, which holds everything together. It contains the buttons and functions of the pot- it is basically the operation base of the Instapot.

Instant Pot Silicone Sealing Ring

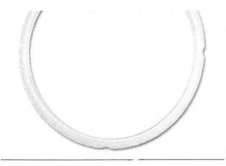

This ring made from silicone prevents air from leaking out of the pot when you close and lock the lid. If buy, any chance you notice steam leaking around the lid, then you have to replace your silicone ring right away (basically, you should replace it every 18 to 24 months).

How to install and remove the Sealing Ring

This is quite easy; just pull down the sealing ring one section at a time starting from the sealing ring rack. To put it back, press it down into the rack part by part- it can be put in with either side facing up.

Inner Pot

The inner pot has a 3 ply bottom which facilitates even heating and has a mirror polished surface for easy cleaning. As great as it is for cooking in the instant pot, you can also use it to store leftovers. The inner pot is very dishwasher safe.

9 inch Instant Pot Tempered Glass Lid

This glass lid is especially amazing when you want to use your Instant Pot for slow cooking. You can also use the lid for other functions such as during the 'Keep Warm' mode or simply storing leftovers with the whole inner pot.

The professional grade glass lid contains a stainless steel rim and a steam release vent. The colorless glass is also enables clear viewing of what's going on in the pot. This accessory is also dishwasher safe.

Instant Pot Silicone Cover

This cover is responsible for creating water- tight and air- tight seal on the Instapot's inner pot. It can also be used for storing leftovers straight inside of the inner pot without having to dirty another container- especially if you don't have the glass lid. It's dishwasher safe too.

Instant Pot Silicone Mitt

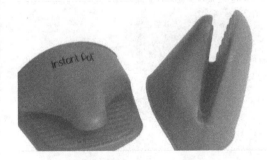

These heat resistant silicone mitts are flexible and easy to put on and off. They have a ridged gripping surface and are non-stick. Always use them when cooking with your Instant Pot to prevent burning- you will feel much safer. The mitts are also dishwasher safe so go ahead and get them dirty!

Soup Spoon

The soupspoon is basically for transferring broth and soup but can also be used as desired. The handle of the spoon hooks onto the inner pot rim.

Measuring cup

The Instapot measuring cup works as a regular cup and can be sued for measuring the quantity of ingredients for your dishes such as multi- grains, rice etc.

Rice paddle

This is used for scooping out food or any other food content. It can both stand up straight or lay flat making it convenient.

Must get Instant Pot accessories

And then there are those accessories that are not included with the Instant Pot out of the box but are totally worth getting. This is simply because they will make everything much easier and isn't that what we all want?

Wide Rim Mesh Basket

This is such a game changer. It can be used as a steamer basket or strainer where you wash your veggies, put them in the basket and add the basket straight into the Inner Pot of the instant pot- fun right?

It saves tons of time particularly when you make something like chicken stock. You can effortlessly take out all ingredients in one move contrary to scooping out little bits at a time.

Note: use pliers to remove both handles to fit the mesh into your Instant Pot.

Instant Pot stainless steel Steam Rack

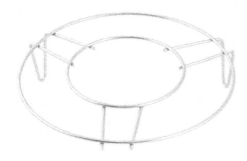

This rack is used in the steaming program to elevate food and keep it away from the water. The handles are designed in such a way that transferring the rack in and out of the inner pot is so easy. It is especially great for PIP recipes and normal steaming on stovetop.

The stainless steel trivet (which is included with the Instant Pot) also performs the same function and can be used in place of the steam rack.

Instant Pot Condensation Cup

This accessory collects any liquid that could possibly come out of the pot. It keeps things less messy.

Steamer Basket

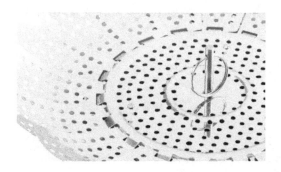

This is 100% premium Stainless Steel. This great steamer basket fits just perfectly in the Instapot. It keeps the veggies and other foods out of the liquid for the required steaming results.

Silicone Steamer Basket

If you are one of those people who prefer to use silicone over using stainless steel then this is a great option for a steamer basket. It is BPA free, really flexible and has nice long handles. Cleaning it is also seamless.

2 Tiers 8 Inches Bamboo Steamer

This is just perfect for dim sum like Har Gow (shrimp dumplings) or Shumai Recipe (pork and shrimp dumplings). Dim sum just tastes better in a bamboo steamer as a bit of the natural bamboo aroma gets infused in the dish while steaming. If you are a fun of dim sum then get this even before you get the instant pot.

For making yogurt:

Greek Yogurt Maker

This BPA free yogurt maker is actually used after you make your homemade instant pot yogurt. It will transform it into a creamy and thick Greek yogurt. The newer version is the Euro Cuisine GY60 Greek Yogurt Maker that includes a stainless steel strainer.

How to handle the parts for cooking prep

1: First step- Open the lid

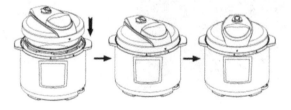

Take the lid handle in your hands and rotate to about 30 degrees counter clockwise until the triangle mark facing downwards on the lid is in line with the same triangle mark facing upwards on the cooker base rim.

2: Check if all the components of the lid are put together properly

Check the pressure release valve and the float valve for any obstructions. Ensure that the sealing ring seats well in its holding rack and that the anti-block shield is placed correctly such that the float valve can move freely.

3: Take out the inner pot and place your foods and liquids in

The total amount of liquids and food should NEVER go past the Max marking. Overfilling the inner pot increases the risk of clogging hence development of excess pressure. This can cause leakage and damage to the unit.

So after ensuring that the lid is in check, add your ingredients to the pot up to the recommended level.

4: Put back the inner pot

First check for any foreign objects inside the cooker base and wipe it dry together with the outside of the inner pot. Place the inner pot into the cooker base and rotate it just a bit to ascertain perfect contact between the heating element and the inner pot.

5: Lock the lid completely

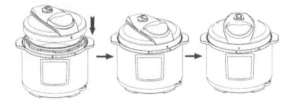

Holding the lead handle, place the lid to cover the cooker with the triangle mark facing downwards on the lid in line with the triangle facing up OPEN mark on the cooker base rim. Rotate the lid clockwise to about 30 degrees until the mark on the lid is in line with the CLOSE mark on the base of the cooker rim. Don't worry; if you don't get it correctly, the Instapot has a safety feature which displays 'Lid' to mean that you haven't positioned the lid correctly.

When using all the programs, the lid should remain closed except when using 'Sauté'. On the 'Keep Warm' and 'Slow Cook' functions, you can work with or without the lid or alternatively use the glass lid.

Place the pressure release handle correctly

You should know that it is perfectly normal for the pressure release handle to be loose. It works with weight and rests on the pressure release outlet. If you need to remove the release handle for washing then simply pull it straight out.

When running any of the functions, except the 'Slow Cook', 'Sauté' and 'Keep Warm', align the pointy end of the release handle to the 'Sealing' position.

Note: If you close the lid during the 'Slow Cook' or 'Keep Warm' functions then you must keep the pressure release valve in the 'Venting' position.

From here, you can choose your program and adjust your functions as desired!

Let's now take the discussion a little further where we will discuss tips and tricks that can make your Instant Pot cooking/using experience an awesome one.

Tips & Tricks to Keep In Mind When Working With Instant Pots

Allow extra cooking time when cooking with frozen ingredients- this gives the ingredients time to thaw.

Be cautious of recipes using flour or dairy- such dishes are not forbidden in the Instapot but you have to be careful and clean the valves and seals once done to avoid food getting stuck there.

Purchase an extra stainless steel insert if using your Instapot frequently- this will help you to not wash as much in between cooking meals.

Never Open the Instant Pot forcefully- Before you attempt to open the instant pot, always make sure that that pressure has been fully released and the floating valve has dropped.

The safest way to open the lid- as you open the lid, tilt it away from you to guide the steam away from you.

Take advantage of PIP (Pot- in Pot) - cooking 2 dishes in an instant pot at the same time will save you even more time and energy. For instance, you can cook chicken at the bottom and rice on top using a steamer rack to lift the rice away from the chicken.

Let's now narrow our discussion to converting normal recipes to Instant Pot recipes.

How to Convert Normal Recipes into Instant Pot Recipes

Time: Start off by knowing the cooking time (and not total time) of the original recipe. Reduce this time by 2/3 for the pressure cooker recipe.

Liquid: Find out the amount of liquid the recipe requires for the finished product (and not which is added). Add only the amount of liquid you need in the finished recipe plus ½ cup extra since pressure cookers don't evaporate much of the extra liquid.

Amount of food: If the original recipe produces a large amount of food, heat it in the pressure cooker in 2 separate batches making sure the cooker isn't more than two thirds full.

For the meat: Coat the bottom of the pressure cooker with about 3 tablespoons of oil before adding any poultry, meat or sea food or else you will miss out on the flavorful outer crust that you normally get when sautéing.

For the rest: Add the fruits, sauces, veggies, pastas or soup ingredients just as you would on the original recipe.

So what do you do after cooking? Well, you clean! Let's learn how to clean the Instant Pot well.

How To Clean Your Instant Pot

Now that the instant pot has done good to you, it's time to pay back- by cleaning it. Luckily, for you, this isn't so hard.

How to generally clean an Instant Pot

What You Need

Small scrub brush

Dishwasher (optional)

Dish soap

Cotton or microfiber cloth

Vinegar

How to do it

1. First unplug the appliance- if you haven't yet.

2. Separate the inner pot and the lid from the housing and clean- wipe the outside of the housing to remove any tough stains and crumbs. For the recessed area of the housing, use a small brush to scrape out dried food residue.

   Caution- the housing/base unit should never be immersed in water as it has electronic components.

3. Use warm soapy water to hand-wash the lid. If you usually allow your Instapot to cool naturally then you will notice that the lid is clean with only condensation water.

   You don't really need to unscrew anything; simply wipe dry using a dry cloth- although you should set a periodic deep clean for the lid where you remove some of the key parts.

4. Pull out the steam release handle gently and check for any food particle- if there are any, scrape them off.

5. Take out the anti-block shield from below the lid and clean the steam valve (which should never be removed). Put back the anti-block shield and use your hands to tighten it.

6. Remove the silicone ring that anchors the float valve and clean then both. Once dry reattach.

7. Remove the sealing ring and clean it by dishwasher or soaking it in vinegar first to eliminate any odors.

8. Clean both the steam rack and inner pot thoroughly.

9. Once done, soak or wipe the Inner Pot with vinegar to remove discoloring.

10. Reassemble all the arts and make sure everything is where it's supposed to be and how it is supposed to be.

How to rid your instant pot of odor

So here is a 'fun' fact; the silicone ring is prone to odors. First off, prevention is better than cure. I found out that keeping the ring open to fresh air by keeping it upside down when you store it or hanging it helps keep it aired. But if you find yourself with odor, then you can get rid of it with the following tips:

Tip #1

Start by soaking the ring in hot soapy water and clean as you remove any food particles. Next, make a paste of water and baking soda and scrub the pot with it.

Lastly, put the ring on the top rack of the dishwasher and run it. You can then place the ring in the sun (if possible) to remove any odors that might have been left behind.

Tip #2

For super savory odors, simply cook white rice in the pot. It will leave a slight rice odor but it works magic.

Tip #3

You can also buy an extra ring and use one for extremely savory foods and meats and the other for bland or sweet foods. Clean them thoroughly too.

With what we have learnt so far, you perhaps are wondering how you will stand to gain after using the Instant Pot.

Why You MUST own an Instant Pot

The benefits of using instant pots are endless making the gadget seem somewhat too good to be true- but once you get your own, you will know what I'm talking about. Here are the reasons why Instapots are so adored worldwide.

Super safe to use

This pot features around 10 in-built safety techs and mechanisms that make it totally safe to use. Some people have a steamy rattling and explosions mentality when it comes to pressure cookers but with an Instapot, safety is guaranteed.

They are super convenient

Everything is fully automated and you don't have to stand there adjusting the heat and watching the timer and take out the food from the heat to prevent overcooking or other things like that. I mean, you can literally toss in your ingredients and walk away- well not right away because you have to set it first.

The unit has a built in microprocessor, which monitors the temperature and pressure in accordance to the amount of food and liquid you have. It even automatically switches to 'Keep Warm' mode for up to 10 hours until you are ready to dig in. To add on that, you can even plan a meal ahead of time and set the pot to cook later for up to 24 hours. If this isn't convenient, then I don't know what is.

Healthier & Tastier Food – especially tender meat

The beauty of an Instant Pot is food that is tender and full of flavor. The food retains more nutrients and is tastier because the cooking time is cut notably and cooking requires less liquid.

An Instapot is especially great at softening up hard pieces of food. I'm talking mouth watering, fall of the bone meat- even if you cook non-defrosted, totally frozen tough meat! Imagine that.

Cooks fast- saving tons of energy and time

If you are a busy person then this will be your top reason to love an Instapot. Do you ever feel like you really want to eat healthy home cooked meals but sadly you can't since you don't have the gift of time? Well, if you do then worry no more; Instapot is here for the rescue.

For instance, when you want to make goat stew, a slow cooker would take about 4 to 8 hours (note: I have nothing against slow cookers) whereas an Instapot would only take 30 to 40 minutes. And lamb stew? Less than 30 minutes! Fall off the bone baby back pork ribs? Less than 25 minutes! I could go on all day but I'm sure you get the drift.

The pot is also very energy efficient as the cooking time is shortened- precisely, it uses up to about 70% less energy than other methods of cooking.

No smell, no sweat, no noise, no steam

Cooking with sweat and heat in the kitchen is fun for nobody. Nothing kills cooking moods like a hot steamy kitchen that feels like a hot sauna room!

For starters, with an Instapot, you can walk away from the kitchen. The pot is also designed in such a way that it cooks without heating up its surroundings. It is fully sealed so even when pressure builds up, there is no steam, no heat, no noise or smell as it cooks. Just complete peace of mind.

It is a 7 in one cooking appliance

This one is a jack-of-all-trades. Its functions range from slow cooking to yogurt making. There's no need to get a rice cooker, yogurt maker or slow cooker when you have an Instapot- it will do all that for you.

This helps simplify the cooking process if you are cooking a number of dishes, which in turn simplifies the cleanup process- as you are operating on one gadget!

Easy and simple to use

I know a 7 in 1 gadget sounds complex to use but it's quite easy- as we have already established. If you are already familiar with the buttons, just put your food in, push them, and relax.

Easy Instant Pot Recipes

So it happens that traveling around the world is one of my passions- China, India, England, you name it. Another passion of mine is exploring new cuisines so I went on a quest where I mixed travelling and exploring cuisines- and what I got was magic.

As much as I love travelling, time is not always on my side as I try to cover as much ground as I can within a short period. This drove me into getting myself an Instant Pot (which cooks super fast). I then went all around looking for easy and simple instant pot recipes for people like me who doesn't have all day to spend in the kitchen and this book was the result. This book contains delectable and simple recipes that will save you tons of time and keep your taste buds happy.

Let us get started with breakfast recipes!

Breakfast Recipes

Rice Pudding

Servings: 6 Prep Time: 5 mins Cooking Time: 20 mins

Ingredients

- 1-teaspoon vanilla extract

- 1/8 teaspoon sea salt

- ¼-cup maple syrup

- ¾ cup heavy cream or coconut cream

- 1-cup basmati rice

- 1 ¼ cups water

- 2 cups milk

Directions

1. Thoroughly rinse the rice in a fine mesh colander and then put the rice in the Instant Pot.

2. Add water, sea salt, milk and maple syrup and stir a bit to mix the ingredients.

3. Close the lid and ensure the vent is closed. Click the porridge function, as this will allow the rice to cook for 20 minutes.

4. Once ready, allow for natural pressure release before opening the lid. Add cream and vanilla and stir.

5. Serve with toppings such as raisins, jam or maple syrup (Optional).

Instant Pot Steel Cut Oats

Servings: 6 Prep Time: 3 mins Cooking Time: 20 mins

PLEASE NOTE: It takes 15-20 minutes to get up to the needed pressure and 20 minutes to make the porridge.

Ingredients

- ½ teaspoon salt

- ¼ cup maple syrup (Optional)

- ½ teaspoon nutmeg

- 1 teaspoon cinnamon

- 1 teaspoon fresh lemon juice

- 2-4 tablespoons butter

- 1 ½ cups fresh cranberries

- 4 apples, diced

- 3 cups water

- 1 cup yogurt

- 2 cups milk or vanilla almond milk (Optional)

- 2 cups steel cut oats

- 2 teaspoons vanilla (Optional)

Directions

1. The night before, apply butter to the bottom of your Instant Pot and add all the ingredients except the vanilla, salt and maple syrup.

   Optional: You can choose to set a delay timer if you want your Steel Cut Oats hot and ready for the morning. If so, add all ingredients except the vanilla. Set a delay timer for 20 minutes before you wake up, allowing the oats to absorb all ingredients overnight and leaving you ready to be served a hot and delicious, oaty meal in the morning.

   Tip: How to set a delay timer

   - Go to the *"Manual" or "Pressure Cooker"* button

   - Adjust the cooking timing with the "+" & "-" buttons

   - Press the *"Delay Start"* or the *"Timer"* button

   - Adjust the delay cooking time (hours/minutes/seconds) with the "+" & "-" buttons

2. In the morning, add the remaining ingredients (do not add the vanilla), close the valve and select the porridge option.

3. Once the desired pressure has reached (15-20 mins), leave to cook for 20 minutes.

4. Once cooking is done, do a quick release. Remove the lid and stir in the vanilla before serving with milk, soothing until creamy and thickened. If you'd like, top with summer fruit of your choosing.

Chinese Rice Porridge

Servings: 2-4 Prep Time: 10 mins Cooking Time: 1 hour

Ingredients

- 2-4 cups shredded cabbage (put at the very end)

- 1-2 tablespoons grated fresh ginger

- 1 - 1 ½ cups short grain rice

- 1/2 to 1 tablespoon coarse unrefined salt (if your broth is salted, use less)

- 6-10 cups homemade bone broth of choice

- 1 pound of ground chicken or ground pork

- 1 tablespoon lard

- 1 onion, diced

- 2-3 radishes, diced

- 1 turnip, peeled and diced

- 3 ribs celery, thinly sliced

- Optional: fish sauce and/or coconut aminos to taste

- Green onions to garnish

Directions

1. Thoroughly rinse the rice until the water is clear.

2. Click the sauté function and then the 'more' option and heat the fat.

3. Add in the onion, radishes, turnip and celery, stir and cook for 3 minutes and the turn off your Instant Pot.

4. Add the chicken or pork, rice, ginger and salt, mix, then pour in the broth, close the lid and vent, and select the porridge function. The cooking process should take about 1 hour.

5. Once the 1-hour elapses, release pressure using quick release, remove the lid, stir the porridge and add in the shredded cabbage. The residual heat should be able to wilt the cabbage.

6. Garnish with green onion and serve with fish sauce or coconut aminos.

Tip: This can be stored in the fridge for up to 5 days. Just reheat it in a pot when you want to eat.

Apple Bread with Caramel Topping

Servings: 8 Prep Time: 10 mins Cooking Time: 1 hour 10 mins

Ingredients

- 1 tablespoon baking powder

- 1 stick butter

- 2 cups flour

- 1 tablespoon apple pie spice

- 1 tablespoon vanilla

- 2 eggs

- 1 cup sugar

- 3 cups apples, peeled, cored and cubed

For the topping:

- 2 cups powdered sugar

- 1 cup heavy cream

- 2 cups brown sugar

- 1 stick butter

Directions

1. Mix the eggs, butter, sugar, vanilla and apple pie spice until creamy and smooth, and then add in the apples.

2. In a separate bowl, mix the flour and baking powder and then add the dry ingredients to the wet ingredients and mix.

3. Once you have mixed all the ingredients, pour the batter into a 7-inch spring form pan.

4. Put the trivet in the instant pot and place 1 cup of water inside the pot. Put the pan on the trivet and cook on manual high for 70 minutes and then do a quick pressure release.

5. Remove the pan from the instant pot, add mixed toppings and serve with a cup of coffee or tea.

Topping:

1. For topping, melt the butter in a saucepan, add the brown sugar then boil for 3 minutes until sugar merges with butter.

2. Add the heavy cream, stirring for 2 ½ minutes until slightly thickened.

3. Remove from heat and let cool. Mingle with powdered sugar and stir, ensuring no lumps.

Vanilla Steel Cut Oats

Servings: 4 Prep Time: 2 mins Cooking Time: 10 mins

Ingredients

- 2 teaspoons vanilla extract

- ¼ teaspoon salt

- 1 teaspoon espresso powder

- 2 tablespoons sugar

- 1 cup steel cut oats

- 1 cup milk

- 2 ½ cups water

- Finely grated chocolate

- Freshly whipped cream

- Maple Syrup (Optional)

- Summer fruits/ Blueberries (Optional)

Directions

1. Place oats, milk, water, salt, sugar and espresso powder in the instant pot and mix well until the powder dissolves and then lock the lid. Cook for 10 minutes at high pressure.

2. Once the 10 minutes elapse, allow for natural pressure release and then do a quick release.

3. Remove the lid and add in sugar and vanilla extract. Cover the instant pot again and allow it to sit for 5 minutes.

4. Serve with grated chocolate, maple syrup and whipped cream if you wish.

Hard Boiled Eggs

Servings: 2 Prep Time: 2 mins Cooking Time: 7 mins

Ingredients

- 4 eggs
- 1 cup water
- 4 slices brown/white bloomer bread (optional)
- Pinch of salt & ground black pepper
- Parsley leaves

Directions

1. Place the eggs in the Instant Pot rack and then add 1 cup of water at the bottom of the pot and close the lid.

2. Use the manual setting and set the time for 7 minutes.

3. After the 7 minutes, do a quick release. Remove the eggs and place them in cool water for a few seconds, peel, then slice equally.

4. Butter the slices of bread, gently place the eggs on top, and then drizzle with a pinch salt & pepper.

5. Garnish with chopped parsley leaves and serve with your favorite vegetables.

Almond Steel Cut Oats

Servings: 4 Prep Time: 3 mins Cooking Time: 10 mins

Ingredients

- ¼ cup sliced almonds
- ¼ cup mini chocolate chips
- ¼ cup toasted shredded coconut
- ¼ teaspoon salt
- 3 ½ cups almond coconut milk
- 1 cup steel cut oats
- 1 tablespoon butter

Directions

1. Place the butter in your Instant pot and click the sauté function.

2. When the butter melts, add the oats and stir constantly for 3 minutes to toast them.

3. Add the milk and salt and cook for 10 minutes on high.

4. Once the time elapses, allow for natural pressure release followed by a quick release.

5. Remove the lid, stir the oats and then let them sit for at least 5 minutes before serving.

6. Top with almonds, chocolate chips or shredded coconut and milk if you wish.

Instant Pot Egg Cupcakes

Servings: 4 Prep Time: 5 mins Cooking Time: 10 mins

Ingredients

- 1 scallion, diced (reserve half)

- ½ cup potatoes, peeled and finely diced

- 1 tablespoon cream

- ½ cup cheese, shredded

- ¼ cup crisp bacon, diced

- ½ teaspoon seasoned salt

- 7 large eggs

Directions

1. Grease 4 half pint (8 oz.) mason jars. In a bowl, mix the eggs, cream and salt and then pour the mixture into the 4 greased mason jars or similar oven proof containers that will fit into your Instant Pot.

2. Next, combine half the scallion, half the cheese, bacon and potatoes and divide them among the 4 containers.

3. Pour 1 cup of water in your Instant Pot and place the trivet inside. Place the jars on the trivet, cook for 5 minutes on high and allow for natural pressure release once the cooking is done.

4. Open the lid and sprinkle the remaining grated cheese on top and then cover the pot again and let it sit for 1 minute.

5. Remove, garnish with scallions and serve.

Pumpkin Porridge

Servings: 4 Prep Time: 5 mins Cooking Time: 15 mins

Ingredients

- 1 cup pumpkin puree
- 2 tablespoons sugar
- 1½ cups oatmeal
- 2 teaspoons pumpkin pie spice
- 1 cup unsweetened almond milk
- 2½ cups water

Directions

1. Place all the ingredients in your Instant Pot and lock the lid. Use the manual setting and set the time for 3 minutes on high.

2. After the 3 minutes, allow the pressure to release naturally. Remove the lid and check the firmness of the porridge. If it is too firm, close the lid and wait for 5-10 minutes for it to achieve the suitable texture.Serve and enjoy.

Crustless Tomato Spinach Quiche

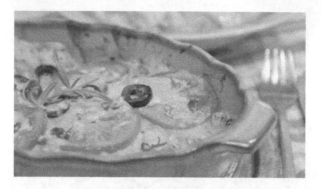

Servings: 6 Prep Time: 5 mins Cooking Time: 20 mins

Ingredients

- ¼ cup shredded parmesan cheese

- 4 tomato slices for topping

- 3 large green onions, sliced

- 1 cup tomato, seeded and diced

- 3 cups fresh baby spinach, roughly chopped

- ¼ teaspoon black pepper

- ½ teaspoon salt

- ½ cup milk

- 12 large eggs

Directions

1. Place the trivet inside the Instant Pot and add 1 ½ cups of water.

2. In a bowl, whisk eggs, salt, pepper and milk.

3. In a baking dish, mix spinach, green onions and tomatoes and then stir in the egg mixture and place pieces of tomatoes on top. Sprinkle cheese over the tomatoes and use a sling to lower the dish to the trivet.

4. Close the lid and use the manual setting to set time for 20 minutes on high.

5. Once time is up, allow for natural pressure release followed by a quick release. Broil the quiche until lightly browned (Optional). Slice and serve.

Lunch Recipes

Italian Sausage and Peppers

Servings: 5 Prep Time: 10 mins Cooking Time: 25 mins

Ingredients

- 1 tablespoon Italian seasoning

- 2 teaspoons garlic powder (or 4 minced cloves)

- 1 tablespoon basil

- 1 cup water

- 1 (15-ounce) can tomato sauce

- 1 (28-ounce) can diced tomatoes

- 4 large green bell peppers, seeded, cored and cut into ½-inch chunks

- 2 19-ounce packages Italian Sausage (10 sausages)

Directions

1. Mix the tomatoes, tomato sauce, garlic powder, basil, Italian seasoning and water in your Instant Pot. Add the sausage on top of the mixture and then the peppers but do not stir.

2. Close the lid and cook for 25 minutes on high.

3. Once the cooking is done, do a quick release. Remove the lid. Serve and enjoy.

Beef Ribs with Thai Sauce

Servings: 4 Prep Time: 10 mins Cooking Time: 65 mins

Ingredients

- 1 tablespoon white sesame seeds

- 2 tablespoons sunflower seed butter

- 1/3 cup coconut aminos

- 2/3 cup bone broth

- ½ teaspoon red pepper flakes (optional)

- 4 garlic cloves, minced

- 1 tablespoon ginger, minced

- 1 medium leek, thinly sliced (use the white and pale green parts)

- 2 pounds bone-in beef short ribs

- 2 tablespoons white sesame seeds

Directions

1. Season the short ribs with salt. Press the sauté function on your Instant Pot and heat oil until hot and then proceed to brown the short ribs for about 8 minutes. Turn the ribs to ensure even browning on both sides before removing them and setting them aside.

2. Place the leeks, garlic, red pepper flakes and ginger inside the Instant pot and cook for 3 minutes stirring occasionally. Add the broth and the sunflower seed butter and stir well to scrap up the browned bits inside the pot.

3. After the 3 minutes are up, return the short ribs to the pot. You should place the meaty part at the bottom such that it is submerged in the broth mixture. Close the lid and set the time for 50 minutes on the manual setting.

4. Allow the pressure to release naturally.

5. Remove the short ribs and slice. Discard the solids from the sauce and serve the meat and sauce with cauliflower rice or zucchini noodles.

Sweet Potato and Red Curry Soup

Servings: 4-6 Prep Time: 7 mins Cooking Time: 10 mins

Ingredients

- 1 can green chilies

- 1 tablespoon lime juice

- ½ cup of cilantro, cut into small pieces

- 28 ounces diced tomatoes, not drained

- 1 (15-ounce) can coconut milk

- 2 tablespoons red curry paste

- 2 (15-ounce) cans of kidney beans, cooked, drained and rinsed

- 4 cups vegetable broth

- 1 teaspoon sea salt

- 1 cup dried brown lentils

- 1 ½ pounds sweet potatoes, diced (you can add more if you wish)

- 2 tablespoons chili powder

- 2 cloves garlic, minced

- 1 large onion

Directions

1. Click the sauté function, heat up olive oil and then add the onion and garlic. Stir a bit and once they soften, add the sweet potatoes and stir to mix the ingredients. Click 'cancel' in order to stop the sauté function.

2. Add the remaining ingredients into your instant pot and then close the lid well. The steam valve should be 'sealed'.

3. Using the manual setting, adjust time to 10 minutes. Once the cooking time elapses, allow the pressure to release naturally and then open the lid. Stir once more and serve while hot.

Thai Chicken and Eggplant

Servings: 6 Prep Time: 5 mins Cooking Time: 10 mins

Ingredients

- 6 Thai basil leaves, julienned

- 12 Thai eggplants, tops removed, cut in half

- ½ cup chicken stock

- 2 tablespoons sugar

- 2 tablespoons fish sauce

- 6 boneless, skinless chicken thighs, cut into 1-2 inch pieces

- 1 can coconut milk

- 3 tablespoons Thai red curry paste

- 1 tablespoon oil

Directions

1. Click on the sauté function; add in the curry paste and 2 tablespoons of coconut milk once the Instant Pot heats up.

2. Add the chicken, stir and sauté for a few minutes before adding the fish sauce, eggplants, the rest of the coconut milk and chicken stock. Close the lid properly and cook on high for 6 minutes.

3. Once the food is ready, allow the pressure to release naturally. Plate the food and garnish with basil leaves. Serve with Jasmine rice or salad.

Chicken Cordon Bleu Casserole

Servings: 4 Prep Time: 10 mins Cooking Time: 25 mins

Ingredients

- 1 cup panko bread crumbs

- 2 tablespoons butter

- 1 tablespoon spicy mustard

- 2 cups chicken broth

- 8 oz. heavy cream

- 8 oz. Gouda cheese

- 16 oz. Swiss cheese

- 1 pound cubed ham

- 1 pound boneless, skinless chicken breast

- 16 oz. Rotini pasta

Directions

1. Place the pasta in the Instant Pot and add the chicken broth. Add ham and chicken strips on top and close the lid. Cook for 25 minutes on manual high. Alternatively, you can use the poultry setting.

2. Once the time elapses, do a quick release. Remove the lid, stir and then add in mustard, cheese and heavy cream mustard. You can melt the butter in a pan and mix it with the breadcrumbs until browned. Sprinkle the mixture on the cordon and serve.

Italian Pulled Pork

Servings: 10 Prep Time: 10 mins Cooking Time: 50 mins

Ingredients

- 1 tablespoon fresh parsley, chopped and divided
- 2 bay leaves
- 2 sprigs fresh thyme
- 1 (7-ounce) jar roasted red peppers, drained
- 1 (28-ounce) can crushed tomatoes
- 5 cloves garlic, smashed
- 1 teaspoon olive oil
- Black pepper to taste
- 1 teaspoon kosher salt
- 18 oz. pork tenderloin

Directions

1. Use salt and pepper to season the pork. Click the sauté function and heat up the oil. Add the garlic and brown for 1-1 ½ minutes before removing the garlic from the instant pot.

2. Place the seasoned pork in your instant pot and brown each side for 2 minutes before adding the garlic, half the parsley and the rest of the ingredients. Cook for 45 minutes on high pressure.

3. Once the time elapses, allow the pressure to release naturally. Remove the bay leaves and then shred the pork using two forks to make your work easier.

4. Top the pork with the remaining parsley and serve with pasta, zucchini noodles or brioche bun.

Mexican Chicken Soup

Servings: 6 Prep Time: 10 mins Cooking Time: 15 mins

Ingredients

- 2 tablespoons juice Lime
- 4 cups cooked and diced boneless chicken breasts
- ½ cup fresh cilantro, chopped
- 2 teaspoons sea salt
- 1 tablespoon chili powder
- 1 teaspoon ground coriander
- 1 tablespoon cumin
- 1 ¾ cups tomato juice
- ¼ cup seeded and diced Jalapeño
- ½ cup diced roma tomato
- 4 teaspoons minced garlic cloves
- ⅔ cup diced red onion

- 1 ½ cups diced carrot

- 6 cups chicken broth/stock

Directions

1. Put all ingredients in your instant pot, lock lid in place and seal the steam nozzle. Select the soup setting and set the time for 10 minutes.

2. After the 10 minutes elapse, pressure release naturally for around 5 minutes and then release any pressure remaining.

3. Once the cooking is done, allow for natural pressure release.

4. Serve with avocado.

Vegetable Beef Stew

Servings: 6 Prep Time: 10 mins Cooking Time: 2 hours

Ingredients

- ½ teaspoon ground oregano

- 2 teaspoons dried parsley flakes

- ½ teaspoon pepper

- ½ teaspoon salt

- 3 tablespoons tomato paste

- 3-4 medium-large potatoes, cut into bite-sized chunks

- 3 stalks of celery, sliced or diced

- 4 carrots, sliced into round disks

- 3 cups beef broth

- 1 (14.5 oz.) can stewed tomatoes, with liquid

- 2 teaspoons garlic, minced

- 1 large onion, diced

- 2 lbs. lean ground beef

Directions

1. Select the sauté function and add the beef, garlic and onion. Cook until the beef is brown and drain the oil as much as possible.

2. Add stewed tomatoes, diced vegetables, beef broth, seasonings and tomato paste and then close the lid and vent. Use the manual setting and set the time for 4 minutes.

3. Once the cooking is done, release the pressure and serve.

Pressure Cooked Pot Roast

Servings: 6 Prep Time: 15 mins Cooking Time: 40 mins

Ingredients

- 2 tablespoons olive oil
- 3 cloves garlic
- 2 tablespoons Italian Seasonings
- 2 stalks chopped celery
- 4 large potatoes in large cubes
- 4 chopped carrots
- 1 cup red wine
- 1 cup beef broth
- 1 onion
- 2-3 pound Chuck Roast
- 3 tablespoons steak sauce (optional)

Directions

1. Click the sauté function and add olive oil to your Instant Pot. Brown the roast for 1-2 minutes on each side.

2. Remove the roast and put the potatoes, celery and carrots inside the instant pot. Add the onions, garlic, beef broth and wine and then place the browned roast on top. Season with steak sauce and close the lid. Use the manual setting and set the time for 35 minutes on high.

3. Once the 35 minutes elapse, do a natural release and serve.

Pasta with Lentil Bolognese

Servings: 6 Prep Time: 5 mins Cooking Time: 15 mins

Ingredients

- 2 tablespoons Italian seasonings, dry
- 4 cups of water
- 1 can tomato paste
- 3 medium carrots, diced
- 4 cloves garlic, minced
- 1 yellow onion, diced
- 1 (28-ounce) can of fire roasted chopped tomatoes
- 1 cup of Beluga black lentils, washed
- Balsamic vinegar (for finishing)
- Salt and pepper to taste
- Red pepper flakes to taste

Directions

1. Place all the ingredients except the salt and balsamic vinegar in the instant pot, lock the lid, use the manual setup and set the time to 15 minutes on high.

2. Once the 15 minutes elapse, allow for natural pressure release and then add a drizzle of balsamic vinegar and salt to taste. Serve with bread or pasta.

Instant Pot Pasta Florentine

Servings: 4 Prep Time: 3 mins Cooking Time: 6 mins

Ingredients

- ¾ cup shredded mozzarella
- 2 cups water
- 1 jar sweet basil pasta sauce
- 1 box penne pasta
- 12 oz bag frozen spinach
- 1 cup sliced mushrooms
- 2 cloves garlic, minced
- 1 diced onion

- 1 pound hot or sweet Italian sausage

- Grated pecorino romano

Directions

1. Click on the sauté function and then brown the garlic, onions, sausages and mushrooms.

2. Once the sausages are browned, add the pasta and frozen spinach and pour in enough water to barely cover the pasta. Cook on high for 6 minutes.

3. Once the cooking time elapses, do a quick manual release, open the lid and stir in the mozzarella. Remove and serve with pecorino Romano cheese.

Chicken Tortilla Soup

Servings: 8 Prep Time: 5 mins Cooking Time: 15 mins

Ingredients

- 1 tablespoon extra-virgin olive oil

- ½ teaspoon chipotle powder

- 1 tablespoon cumin

- 1 tablespoon chili powder

- 1 teaspoon minced garlic

- ½ bunch cilantro, chopped finely

- 1 bell pepper, diced

- 1 medium onion, diced

- 4 cups chicken stock, no salt added

- 2 cans petite diced tomatoes, drained

- 2 cans of beans, drained and NOT rinsed

- 3 chicken breasts (1.5 lbs.)

- Kosher salt and pepper to taste

Directions

1. Click the sauté function and add the olive oil. Once hot, add the bell peppers, onions, and sauté for 4-5 minutes and then add the salt, pepper and garlic and cook for 2 more minutes.

2. Add tomatoes and beans and stir well to mix. Add more salt (1 teaspoon) and ground pepper (1/2 teaspoon) and stir. Place the chicken breasts on top, add the chicken stock and cilantro, and then close the lid. Cook for 8 minutes using the manual setting.

3. Once ready, do a quick release. Remove chicken and shred before putting it back inside the pot. Adjust salt and pepper and mix the ingredients.

4. Remove and serve with tortilla chips, avocado, cheese and sour cream if you wish.

Tiger Prawn Risotto

Servings: 2-4 Prep Time: 5 mins Cooking Time: 1 hr 10 mins

Ingredients

- 5 grams Parmesan cheese, finely grated (for garnish)

- 1-2 stalks green onions, thinly sliced

- 20g Parmesan cheese, finely grated

- ½ teaspoon kosher salt

- 1/8 teaspoon baking soda

- ½ pound tiger prawns or shrimp, frozen, unpeeled

- 4 cups homemade fish stock

- 2 ½ tablespoons yellow or white miso paste

- 2 teaspoons Japanese soy sauce

- ¾ cup cooking sake

- 2 cups Arborio rice

- 3 medium cloves garlic, minced

- 1 medium shallot, minced

- 4 tablespoons unsalted butter

- 3 tablespoons olive oil

- Parmesan cheese (5g), finely grated

Directions

1. Click the sauté function on the Instant Pot and once hot, add in the olive oil and butter. Spread this so that it coats the bottom of the pot.

2. Add garlic, shallots and sauté until they are soft before adding the tiger prawns and cooking for 1 more minute. Remove the prawns from the Instant Pot.

3. Place the rice into the pot and stir from time to time for 2-3 minutes to coat with the oil. Add the soy sauce and miso paste and stir.

4. Pour in the cooking sake and ensure you deglaze the bottom of the pot using a wooden spoon so that no bits stick to the pot. Stir for 1 minute, pour in the fish stock, close the lid and cook for 5 minutes on high.

5. Once the cooking time elapses, do a quick release. If the risotto is too runny, cook for a few more minutes on the sauté setting. Add in sliced green onions and parmesan cheese; season with salt and black pepper.

6. Peel the tiger prawns, place them on top of the risotto and serve. You can add more parmesan cheese if you like.

Broccoli Rabe and Chickpeas

Servings: 2-3 Prep Time: 5 mins Cooking Time: 5 mins

Ingredients

- Salt to taste
- ¼ cup water or vegetable broth
- 1 (15-oz) can chickpeas, drained
- 1 bunch broccoli rabe, halved
- 1/8 teaspoon fennel seeds (optional)
- Crushed red pepper to taste
- 3 large cloves of garlic, chopped
- ½ teaspoon olive oil (optional)

Directions

1. Select the sauté function on your instant pot and then add the olive oil and garlic and sauté for a few minutes until they are browned. If you don't want to use oil, you can sauté the garlic with a little water to prevent sticking.

2. Add the fennel seeds and red pepper and let them cook for 30 seconds before adding in the broccoli rabe, vegetable broth and chickpeas. Lock the lid and cook for 3-4 minutes on high.

3. Once the time elapses, do a quick release. Remove and serve. If there is excess water, you can continue cooking using the sauté function until the liquid evaporates. Do not lock your instant pot for this.

Instant Pot Brazilian Potato Salad

Servings: 6-8 Prep Time: 5 mins Cooking Time: 10 mins

Ingredients

- 1 cup corn kernels (fresh or thawed frozen)

- 1 cup green peas (fresh or thawed frozen)

- 1 ½ cup diced carrots

- 2 cups water

- 4 cups Idaho potatoes, cut into bite-sized pieces

Dressing

- ½ teaspoon ground black pepper

- ½ teaspoon salt

- 10 black or green olives, minced

- ¼ cup plus 1 tablespoon vegan mayo

Directions

1. Place the potatoes, carrots and water in the instant pot, and using the manual setup, cook for 10 minutes on high.

2. Allow the pressure to release naturally before removing the lid and adding the peas and corn. Replace the lid and cook for 0 (zero) minutes on low.

3. Once cooking is done, release the pressure manually. Place everything in a colander and rinse to stop the cooking process and then set aside.

4. Mix the dressing ingredients, add them to the cooled vegetables, and mix well. Serve. Chill for an hour before serving (Optional).

Instant Pot Brazilian Chicken Soup

Servings: 4 Prep Time: 5 mins Cooking Time: 25 mins

Ingredients

- Salt and pepper to taste

- 6-7 cups water or chicken stock

- 1 bunch parsley

- Extra virgin oil

- 1 large potato, peeled and thinly diced

- 2 carrots, peeled and thinly diced

- ½ onion, thinly diced

- ½ cup rice

- ½ chicken breast, cut in small cubes or strips

Directions

1. Click the sauté function and heat up the oil. Add the onion, carrots, potato, chicken and rice, and cook for 2 minutes stirring from time to time.

2. Add the parsley and water and close the lid. Cook for 8 minutes on high.

3. After the 8 minutes, release the pressure and check the food. If it is not done, you can add 1 more cup and continue cooking for a few minutes.

4. Season with salt and pepper and serve.

Vegan Feijoada

Servings: 2-4 Prep Time: 10 mins Cooking Time: 40 mins

Ingredients

- 2 ½ cups vegetable broth or water

- 1 spicy vegan sausage, chopped

- 2 bay leaves

- 1/3 cup dry red wine

- ½ teaspoon ground black pepper

- ½ tablespoon Liquid Smoke

- ½ tablespoon smoked paprika

- ½ tablespoon dried thyme

- 1 tablespoon cumin

- 4 cloves garlic, minced

- 1 large red bell pepper, chopped

- 2 large carrots, peeled and cut into circles

- 2 large onions, sliced into half moons

- 1 cup soy curls, softened in hot water, drained

- 2 cups dried black beans, soaked, rinsed and drained

Directions

1. Click the sauté function and add some water or vegetable broth into your Instant Pot and then add the carrots, bell pepper, onions and garlic and stir from time to time for 5 minutes.

2. Add the black pepper and cumin and cook for 1 more minute. Add the wine and continue cooking for 1-2 minutes before adding the sausage, black beans, bay leaves, soy curls and broth. Stir to mix the ingredients together. Close the lid and change the setting to Bean/Chile button and set time for 30 minutes.

3. Once ready, release the pressure. Check the beans to make sure they are done. If not, cook for a few more minutes.

4. Serve with avocado, cilantro and onions.

Mexican Rice

Serves 3 Prep Time: 5 mins Cooking Time: 15 mins

Ingredients

- Salt and freshly ground pepper to taste

- ¼ cup green salsa or green hot sauce

- ½ cup fresh cilantro

- Flesh of ½ large ripe avocado

- 1 cup uncooked long-grain rice

- 1 ¼ cups low-sodium chicken or vegetable broth

Directions

1. Place the rice and broth inside your Instant Pot, stir, lock the lid in place, select high pressure and set the time for 3 minutes.

2. When the beep goes off, allow for natural pressure release before doing a quick release.

3. Open the lid and use a fork to fluff the rice and let it rest as you blend the avocado, salsa, cilantro and a bit of water in a blender to make the sour cream.

4. Add the cream into the rice, season with salt and pepper and stir, then serve.

Cabbage Roll Soup

Servings: 6 Prep Time: 10 mins Cooking Time: 25 mins

Ingredients

- 1 tablespoon oil

- Salt and pepper to taste

- 1 bay leaf

- 1 teaspoon cayenne pepper

- 1 teaspoon thyme

- 1 teaspoon oregano

- 1 tablespoon garlic powder

- 1 tablespoon onion powder

- 1 tablespoon Worcestershire sauce

- 1 ½ cups vegetable juice

- 4 cups beef broth

- 2 tablespoons tomato paste

- 1 (28 oz.) can diced tomatoes, undrained

- 1 medium cabbage, core removed and diced

- ¾ cup uncooked rice

- ½ lb. ground pork

- 1 lb. ground beef

- 3 cloves garlic, minced

- 1 large onion, diced

Directions

1. Select the sauté function and add the oil into your Instant Pot. Add the onions and sauté for 3 minutes before adding the garlic. Stir and add the beef and ground pork and brown them on both sides.

2. Drain the fat, add the remaining ingredients into the instant pot and stir. Lock the lid in place, seal the valve and select 20 minutes cook time.

3. Once ready, serve and enjoy.

Lasagna Soup

Servings: 4-6 Prep Time: 10 mins Cooking Time: 20 mins

Ingredients

- 1 teaspoon oregano

- 1 teaspoon black pepper

- ½ teaspoon onion powder

- ½ - ¾ box of lasagna noodles (break them up)

- 2 cups water

- 4 cups vegetable stock

- 1 large can diced tomatoes, ½ diced, ½ blended

- 2 cups ground veggies (or ground meat)

- 1 small summer squash chopped

- 2 carrots, chopped

- ½ green pepper, chopped

- 1 medium onion, chopped

- 2 tablespoons extra-virgin olive oil

- Optional: pepperoncini and/or chili flakes

- Sea salt, to taste

Directions

1. Put on your instant pot and select the sauté function. Add the oil, carrots, green pepper and onions and sauté for 5-8 minutes or until the onions are golden brown.

2. Add ground veggies and the summer squash and cook for another 2-3 minutes before adding spices and stirring.

3. Add tomatoes, water, broth and lasagna noodles. Press cancel then select manual and set the time to 4 minutes.

4. Once ready, allow for a natural pressure release. Alternatively, do a quick release after 5 minutes. Serve and top with sour cream or shredded cheese if you wish.

Cream Cheese Chicken Chilli

Servings: 4 Prep Time: 10 mins Cooking Time: 40 mins

Ingredients

- 1 packet dry ranch seasoning

- 1 lb. boneless skinless chicken breasts

- 1 can rotel (not drained)

- 1 can corn (not drained)

- 1 can black beans (drained and rinsed)

- Roughly 2 teaspoons of both cumin and chili powder

Directions

1. Place all the ingredients inside the Instant Pot and cook on high for 20 minutes.

2. Once cooking is done, allow for natural pressure release and then remove the chicken.

3. Remove the chicken from the pot to shred it. Break up about 8 oz. of cheese and spread it over the ingredients in the Instant Pot, stir, close the lid and allow it to melt.

4. Put the shredded chicken inside the pot and stir. Once heat through, remove from the heat and serve over rice.

Hamburger Soup

Servings: 6 Prep Time: 5 mins Cooking Time: 12 mins

Ingredients

- 796ml can diced tomatoes

- 4 cups of beef broth

- 4 cups vegetable broth

- 1 ½ cups of small noodles

- 1 onion, finely chopped

- 3 stalks of celery

- 1lb. ground beef

- 4 carrots

- 1 bay leaf

- Italian seasoning

- Splash of Worcestershire sauce

Directions

1. Select the sauté function. Add some vegetable oil and Worcestershire sauce and brown the beef for a few minutes.

2. Add the vegetables and cook for 2-3 minutes before adding the remaining ingredients. Close the lid and select the soup button.

3. Once ready, serve.

No Noodle Lasagne

Servings: 8 Prep Time: 10 mins Cooking Time: 45 mins

Ingredients

- 8 ounces mozzarella sliced

- 1 (25 oz.) jar marinara sauce

- 1 large egg

- ½ cup Parmesan cheese

- 1 ½ cups ricotta cheese

- 1 small onion

- 2 cloves garlic minced

- 1 pound ground beef

Directions

1. Select the sauté function and sauté garlic and onion and ground beef until the beef is browned. In the meantime, mix Parmesan, ricotta cheese and 1 egg in a bowl.

2. Add marinara sauce and mix then remove half of the meat sauce, and then top the remaining meat sauce in the pan with half the mozzarella cheese.

3. Add half of the ricotta cheese mix and then top up with the remaining meat sauce. Spread some mozzarella on top but leave some for the final stage.

4. Add the remaining ricotta cheese mix and then the left over mozzarella cheese. You can use aluminum foil to cover the lasagna if you wish and then cover and cook for 8-10 minutes on high.

5. Once cooking is done, release the pressure, remove the lid and place any remaining cheese on top. Cover the Instant Pot to allow the cheese to melt. Serve and enjoy.

Mexican Rice

Servings: 4-6 Prep Time: 10 mins Cooking Time: 20 mins

Ingredients

- 1 cup shredded cheese

- 2 tablespoons fresh cilantro, chopped

- 1 cup cooked corn kernels

- 15 ounces black beans, rinsed and drained

- 2 cups chunky salsa

- 2 cups water

- 1 cup long grain white rice, rinsed and drained

- ½ teaspoon salt

- ½ teaspoon ground cumin

- 1 teaspoon chili powder

- 1 cup diced red onion

- 1 pound lean ground beef

- 1 tablespoon olive oil

- Boston lettuce (optional for serving)

Directions

1. Select the sauté function and heat the oil. Add ground beef, cumin, onion, salt and chili powder and sauté for 5 minutes stirring occasionally to crumble the beef.

2. Add the rice, salsa and water and stir to mix the ingredients and then close the lid. Cook for 8 minutes on high.

3. Do a quick release and open the Instant Pot. Set it back to the sauté function and add in the corn, black beans and cilantro. Cook for 3 minutes stirring from time to time.

4. Transfer to serving dish, top up with cheese and serve while hot. If you wish, place the food on lettuce leaves to make tasty lettuce wraps.

Multigrain Rice

Servings: 6-8 Prep Time: 5 mins Cooking Time: 60 mins

Ingredients

- 1 ½ teaspoons salt (optional)

- 3 ¾ - 4 ½ cups of water

- 2 tablespoon of oil (olive oil preferred)

- 3 cups brown rice, wild rice or other whole grains, rinsed

Directions

1. Mix all the ingredients and place them in your Instant Pot. Click on the Multigrain function. Once ready, let the rice rest for 5 minutes.

2. Open the lid, and use a wooden spoon to fluff up the grains. Serve with beef and your favorite vegetables.

Sweet Potato with Italian Turkey Sausage

Servings: 4-6 Prep Time: 10 mins Cooking Time: 20 mins

Ingredients

- ½ cup chicken broth

- 2 medium sweet potatoes, peeled and cut into ½ inch chunks

- ¼ teaspoon ground cayenne

- ½ teaspoon salt

- ½ teaspoon dried sage

- ½ teaspoon mild paprika

- ½ teaspoon ground cumin

- ¼ cup shelled green pumpkin seeds

- ½ cup dried cranberries

- ½ small red onion, chopped

- ¾ pound bulk mild Italian turkey sausage (remove casings)

- 2 tablespoons unsalted butter

Directions

1. Select the sauté function on your Instant Pot, add the butter and melt. Add onions and crumbled sausages and sauté until the sausages are browned. This should take about 5 minutes.

2. Add the pumpkin seeds, cranberries, sage, cayenne, paprika, cumin and salt and cook for about 1 minute stirring from time to time. Add the sweet potatoes and continue cooking for 1 more minute before adding the broth. Lock the lid and cook at high pressure for 8 minutes.

3. Do a quick release, remove the lid and select the sauté function and continue cooking for 3-4 minutes or until the liquid evaporates.

4. Serve and enjoy.

Dal Makhani

Servings: 4 Prep Time: 15 mins Cooking Time: 85 mins

Ingredients

- 2 tablespoons ghee or grass-fed butter (add more to taste)

- 3 cups water

- 2 tomatoes, chopped

- ½ teaspoon black pepper

- 1 teaspoon salt, adjust to taste

- 1 teaspoon garam masala

- 1 teaspoon cayenne, adjust to heat preference

- 1 teaspoon turmeric

- 1 ½ inch ginger, minced

- 6 garlic cloves, minced

- 1 bay leaf

- 1 large onion, chopped

- 1 tablespoon cumin seeds

- 2 tablespoons avocado oil

- 1 cup whole and split lentils, soaked in water overnight

- Cilantro leaves, optional

Directions

1. Soak lentils for 24 hours and then drain the water.

2. Select the sauté function, heat the oil and add cumin seeds and sauté until they start to splutter before adding the onion and bay leaf and cook for 8-10 minutes.

3. Add the spices, ginger, garlic, stir, and then add the tomatoes and sauté for 5 more minutes.

4. Add lentils and water and mix together and then lock the lid. Press the Cancel/Keep Warm button, and then press the Bean/Chili option and the food will cook for 30 minutes.

5. After the 30 minutes, allow for natural pressure release. Open the lid, add ghee, stir, then garnish with cilantro, and serve.

Instant Pot Saag

Servings: 4-6 Prep Time: 10 mins Cooking Time: 20 mins

Ingredients

- ½ teaspoon black pepper
- ½ teaspoon cayenne
- ½ teaspoon turmeric
- 1 teaspoon garam masala
- 1 teaspoon cumin
- 1 teaspoon coriander
- 2 *teaspoons* salt
- 4 garlic cloves, minced
- 2-inch knob ginger, minced
- 2 medium onions, diced
- 2 tablespoons ghee (plus extra for serving)

- 1 pound mustard leaves, rinsed

- 1 pound spinach, rinsed

- Pinch of dried fenugreek leaves

Directions

1. Select the sauté function and melt the ghee. Add the onion, spices and garlic and cook for 2-3 minutes.

2. Once the onion is translucent, add spinach and stir. Once the spinach wilts, add the mustard greens and close the lid. Press the keep warm/cancel button. Click the poultry button and this will automatically set the time to 15 minutes.

3. Once ready, allow for natural pressure release. You can blend the contents for a smoother soup and top up with ghee before serving with some bread.

Chicken Congee

Servings: 6 Prep Time: 10 mins Cooking Time: 35 mins

Ingredients

- 1 liter of boiled water

- 1 chicken stock cube

- Big piece of ginger (3-4 inches long), minced

- 2 cups of uncooked rice

- 6-8 medium chicken pieces

Directions

1. Place rice, boiled water, chicken and ginger in the Instant Pot and click the Meat setting to cook for 32 minutes on high.

2. Once ready, allow for natural pressure release. Serve with soy sauce, egg salad and onion if you wish.

Instant Pot Congee

Servings: 6 Prep Time: 10 mins Cooking Time: 30 mins

Ingredients

- ½ tablespoon salt (or to taste)

- 7 cups water

- 2 lb. bone-in chicken pieces

- 3 shitake mushrooms

- 1-2 inches fresh ginger

- 2 cloves garlic

- 1 cup uncooked jasmine rice

- *Toppings:*

- 1 tablespoon toasted sesame oil

- 1 tablespoon soy sauce

- ⅓ cup peanuts, chopped

- 3 green onions, sliced

- ¼ bunch cilantro (optional)

Directions

1. Place the rice in the Instant Pot and add the garlic, mushrooms, ginger, chicken and aromatics on top and then add water and lock the lid. Ensure the steam release valve is set to the "sealing" position and then press the porridge option. The cooking time will be 20 minutes.

2. After the 20 minutes, allow for natural pressure release, remove the chicken and shred it before returning it to your Instant Pot.

3. Add salt if needed and ladle the soup into bowls. Top up with soy sauce, cilantro leaves, toasted sesame oil and peanuts and serve.

Instant Pot Veggie Stew

Servings: 8-10 Prep Time: 30 mins Cooking Time: 15 mins

Ingredients

Sauté mode:

- ½ teaspoon rubbed sage

- 1 teaspoon rosemary

- 1 teaspoon Italian seasoning

- 8oz. sliced portabella mushrooms

- 8oz. white mushrooms

- ¼ cup Veg Broth

- 2 garlic cloves, minced

- 1 carrot, minced

- 1 celery stalk, minced

- ½ onion, minced

Manual mode:

- ¼ teaspoon ground pepper

- ½ teaspoon salt

- 1 tablespoon balsamic vinegar

- 2 Yukon gold potatoes, diced

- 1 cup fresh green beans, diced

- 1 celery stalk, diced

- 2 carrots, diced

- 3 cups vegetable broth

- 8oz tomato sauce

- 15oz. diced tomatoes

- ½ cup red wine

Keep warm mode:

- 2 tablespoons corn starch

- 4oz. frozen peas

- ¾ cup pearl onions

Directions

1. Press the sauté option and select LESS and proceed to sauté the onion, garlic, carrot and celery until the onion is translucent.

2. Add sage, Italian seasoning, rosemary and mushrooms and continue cooking until the liquid evaporates.

3. Use red wine to deglaze the pan before adding tomatoes, sauce, veggie broth and the other veggies except the peas and pearl onions.

4. Add the seasoning and then close the lid and set valve to seal. Using the manual setting, set the time to 15 minutes.

5. Once ready, release the pressure. Open the lid, add peas, corn starch and pearl onions, and stir before serving.

Carne Guisada

Servings: 4 Prep Time: 20 mins Cooking Time: 60 mins

Ingredients

- 1 tablespoon potato starch or thickener of choice

- ½ cup tomato sauce

- 1 cup beef broth or chicken stock

- ½ teaspoon oregano

- ½ teaspoon chipotle powder

- ½ teaspoon pepper

- 1 teaspoon salt

- 1 teaspoon paprika

- 1 teaspoon chili powder

- 1 teaspoon ground cumin

- 1 bay leaf

- 1 Serrano peppers, minced

- 1 tablespoon minced garlic

- 1 onion, diced

- 1 pound beef stew meat

- 2 tablespoons avocado oil or fat of choice

Directions

1. Select the sauté function and heat some oil then add beef and cook for a few minutes until browned.

2. Add the onion, spices, bay leaf, garlic and Serrano pepper and cook for 2-3 minutes. Add the tomato sauce, beef broth, and lock the lid. Click on the meat/stew option and ensure that the steam valve is closed. This will set the time for 35 minutes.

3. Once ready, allow for natural pressure release, stir in the potato starch thickener and serve with tortilla or cauliflower rice if you desire.

Green Bean Casserole

Servings: 4 Prep Time: 10 mins Cooking Time: 30 mins

Ingredients

- ½ cup French Onions for garnish on top

- 16 oz. green beans

- 2 tablespoons butter

- 1 small onion

- 12 oz. sliced mushroom

- 1 cup heavy cream

- 1 cup chicken broth

Directions

1. Press the sauté function and melt the butter. Add the onion and mushrooms into the Instant Pot and sauté for 2-3 minutes.

2. Add chicken broth, green beans and heavy cream. Cook for 15 minutes on manual high pressure.

3. Once ready, do a quick release. Open the lid and add 1-2 tablespoons of corn starch to make it thicker. Garnish with French onion and serve.

Instant Pot Cauliflower and Sweet Potato

Servings: 8 Prep Time: 10 mins Cooking Time: 25 minutes

Ingredients

- 1 tablespoon natural peanut butter

- ¼ teaspoon cayenne pepper (or to taste)

- 1 teaspoon salt (or to taste)

- 2-4 cups water

- 1 (15 oz.) can diced tomatoes

- 1 (15 oz.) can chickpeas, rinsed and drained

- 1 large head cauliflower, separated into bite-sized flowerets

- 1/8 teaspoon cinnamon

- 1 tablespoon mild curry powder, divided

- 1 pound sweet potatoes peeled and cubed

- 4 cups vegetable broth

- 3 cloves garlic, minced

- 1 small chili pepper, seeded and minced

- 1 tablespoon ginger paste or minced ginger root

- ½ teaspoon cumin seeds

- 1 large onion, peeled and chopped

Directions

1. Select the sauté function and sauté onions for 3-4 minutes before adding the cumin seeds, garlic, chili pepper and ginger and cook for 30 seconds stirring from time to time.

2. Add the broth, cinnamon, sweet potatoes and 1 teaspoon curry powder and close the lid. Use the manual or high-pressure setting and set the time for 4 minutes on high.

3. After the time elapses, do a quick release and select the sauté function. Add cauliflower, tomatoes and chickpeas, 3 cups of water, cayenne pepper, 2 teaspoons curry powder and salt and cook until the cauliflower is tender.

4. Add peanut butter and serve.

Veggie Soup

Servings: 14 Prep Time: 10 mins Cooking Time: 10 mins

Ingredients

- ½ tablespoon garlic powder

- 2 teaspoons dried basil

- 2 teaspoons dried oregano

- ¼ - ½ teaspoon cayenne powder

- 1 teaspoon cumin powder

- 1 tablespoon onion powder

- ½ tablespoon paprika

- 3 tablespoons chili powder

- 3-5 garlic cloves, chopped

- 1 onion, chopped

- 1 large sweet potato (or potato of choice)

- 4-8 oz. sliced mushrooms

- 12 oz. frozen bag of Mexican style vegetables

- 12 oz. frozen bag of Italian style vegetables

- 12 oz. frozen bag of chopped spinach

- 14.5 oz. can tomato sauce

- 14.5 oz can diced tomatoes

- 15 oz. can hot chili beans

- 15 oz. can kidney beans (rinsed and drained)

- 4 cups vegetable broth

- Bay leaf (optional), discard when soup is ready

Directions

1. Place all the ingredients in your Instant pot and lock the lid. Click the soup option and reduce the time to 10 minutes.

2. Once ready, allow for natural pressure release. Serve and enjoy.

Dinner Recipes

Mexican Polenta

Servings: 3 Prep Time: 10 mins Cooking Time: 15 mins

Ingredients

- ¼ teaspoon cayenne pepper (optional)

- ½ teaspoon smoked paprika

- 1 teaspoon oregano

- 1 teaspoon cumin

- 1 tablespoon chili powder

- ¼ cup fresh cilantro, chopped

- 1 cup corn meal/grits

- 2 cups boiling water

- 2 cups vegetable broth

- 2 teaspoons minced garlic

- 1 bunch sliced green onion (approx. one cup, greens and whites)

Directions

1. Press the sauté function, add a bit of water and cook the onions and garlic for 2-4 minutes.

2. Add vegetable broth, corn meal, spices, boiling water and cilantro and stir before locking the lid. Use the manual setting and set the time for 5 minutes on high.

3. Once ready, allow for natural pressure release. Stir and serve with some beef.

Instant Pot Chile Verde

Servings: 4 Prep Time: 10 mins Cooking Time: 30 mins

Ingredients

- About 1 cup green salsa

- 1 pound of pork, cut chunks the size of stew meat

- 1 onion, diced

- 2 garlic cloves, minced

- 1 teaspoon cumin

- Salt and pepper to taste

Directions

1. Select the sauté function and brown the pork, onion and garlic. Add the salsa, cumin and click on the Meat/Stew setting to cook for 20-30 minutes.

2. Once ready, allow the pressure to release. Serve over rice with your favorite vegetables.

Mexican Casserole

Servings: 4-6 Prep Time: 10 mins Cooking Time: 30 mins

Ingredients

- 1 teaspoon sea salt (optional)
- 2 teaspoons chili powder
- 2 teaspoons onion powder
- 1 teaspoon garlic
- 1 (6 oz.) can of tomato paste (or 1 8 oz can tomato sauce with slightly less water)
- 5 cups water
- 1 cup uncooked dry beans
- 2 cups uncooked brown rice

Directions

1. Place all the ingredients in your Instant Pot, stir to mix and lock the lid. Use the manual setting and set the time for 28 minutes.

2. After the time elapses, allow for natural pressure release.

3. Serve alone or with tortillas.

Instant Pot Pork and Hominy stew

Servings: 6-8 Prep Time: 15 mins Cooking Time: 40 mins

Ingredients

- 1 fresh red bell pepper

- 3 teaspoons salt

- 1 teaspoon cumin powder

- 3 cloves garlic, divided

- 1 teaspoon dried Mexican Oregano, crumbled

- 2 dried ancho chilies, stems removed and seeded

- 2 bay leaves

- 2 lbs. boneless pork (leg, shoulder or neck), sliced in large 2" chunks

- 4 cups water

- 2 cups dry hominy kernels, soaked overnight

To Garnish:

- Lime wedges

- A wedge of cabbage, thinly sliced

- A cubed avocado

- Thinly sliced radishes

Directions

1. Place the hominy and water in your Instant Pot and lock the lid. Cook on high for 15 minutes and then allow the pressure to release before adding the meat, oregano, bay leaves, cumin powder, ancho chilies, garlic and salt and then close the lid. Cook on high for 10 minutes.

2. After the 10 minutes, allow for natural pressure release. Open the lid and discard the bay leaves. Fish out 2 tablespoons of hominy and the ancho chilies and puree them and then return them to the Instant Pot and continue cooking uncovered for 5-10 minutes.

3. Serve and garnish with lime wedges.

Instant Pot Mexican Rice

Servings: 4-6 Prep Time: 10 mins Cooking Time: 20 mins

Ingredients

- 1 green onion, chopped (optional)

- 1 teaspoon oregano

- 2 teaspoons salt

- 2½ cups water

- 1 cup chopped tomatoes and their juice or canned chopped tomatoes

- 2 cups medium or long grain white rice

- 1 onion, chopped

- ⅛ teaspoon cayenne pepper

- 1 tablespoon vegetable oil

Directions

1. Select the sauté function, add the vegetable oil and sauté the onions for 3-5 minutes or until they soften and then add the rice and continue cooking for 3 more minutes.

2. Add the tomatoes, oregano, cayenne pepper, water and salt and stir to mix and then close the lid. Cook on high for 4-5 minutes.

3. Once cooking is done, allow for natural pressure release and then do a quick release. Open the lid, fluff the rice, garnish with green onion and serve.

Instant Pot Braised Beef

Servings: 6 Prep Time: 20 mins Cooking Time: 45 mins

Ingredients

- 1lb. beef shank

Marinade:

- 3 tablespoons light soy sauce

- 1 teaspoon sugar

- 1 teaspoon salt

- 2 teaspoons pepper cones

Sauce:

- 5 cups water

- 2 chopped green onions

- 5g fresh ginger shredded

- 2 teaspoons sesame oil

- 1 tablespoon Jasmine green tea

- 2 bay leaves

- 1 ½ teaspoon cumin

- 2 anises

- 3 clovers

- 3 tablespoons dark soy sauce

- ½ cup light soy sauce

- 2 teaspoons sugar

- 2 teaspoons salt

Directions

1. Mix the marinade ingredients in a bowl then pour into a zip-lock bag. Place the beef in the zip-lock bag, toss to coat and put in the fridge to marinate for a few hours.

2. When ready to use, rinse off pepper cones and then place the beef and sauce ingredients in your Instant Pot. Lock the lid, ensuring the valve is in the seal position. Press manual button and set the timer to 35 minutes.

3. Once the time is up, allow for natural pressure release, remove the beef shank and let it rest in a container for a few minutes, slice and serve.

Rice with Sausage

Servings: 8 Prep Time: 15 mins Cooking Time: 30 mins

Ingredients

- 1 tablespoon finely chopped green onion

- ¼ teaspoon chicken broth mix

- 1/6 teaspoon ground black pepper

- 3 cups water

- 1 teaspoon salt

- 2 cups long grain rice

- 3-4 slices of fresh ginger

- 1 ½ tablespoon finely chopped green onion

- 1 ½ tablespoon olive oil

- 5 small yellow potatoes, peeled

- 2 lean Chinese sausages, thinly sliced

Directions

1. Pour in the olive oil in the Instant Pot and press the sauté function and adjust to 'more'. Add ginger and green onions and sauté for 2 minutes before adding the sausages and cooking for 1-2 minutes.

2. Add the potatoes and continue cooking for another 1-2 minutes before adding the rice and stirring to combine. Add the remaining ingredients and cover the lid. Make sure the valve is in seal position and then click the rice option.

3. Once ready, allow the pressure to release naturally and then let the rice rest for 5 more minutes before opening the lid. Garnish with green onion and serve.

Instant Pot Beef and Broccoli Stir-fry

Servings: 2-4 Prep Time: 25 mins Cooking Time: 25 mins

Ingredients

- 1 tablespoon Shaoxing wine

- 3 cloves garlic, minced

- 1 tablespoon ginger, minced

- 1 tablespoon peanut oil

- 1 tablespoon salt

- 1 tablespoon corn starch

- 1 head broccoli, chopped into large florets

- 1 pound flank steak, sliced thinly against the grain

Stir Fry Sauce:

- A dash of sesame oil

- ¼ teaspoon sugar

- ⅓ teaspoon five spice powder

- 1 teaspoon Shaoxing wine

- ½ tablespoon oyster sauce

- 1 tablespoon vegetable oil

- 1 tablespoon dark soy sauce

- 2 tablespoons light soy sauce

- 5 tablespoons water

Directions

1. Use corn starch and 2/3 of the stir-fry sauce ingredients to marinate the beef for at least 20 minutes.

2. Place the broccoli in boiling water for a minute in order to blanch it. Drain and set aside.

3. Select the sauté function and adjust to 'more'. Once the pot is hot, add peanut oil and put in the marinated beef. Cook until 80% done before removing and setting aside.

4. Add 1 tablespoon of peanut oil, ginger and garlic into the pot and cook for 30 seconds as you stir. Then add the broccoli and stir. Cook for 1 more minute before returning the beef into the pot. Add the wine and stir and then add the remaining stir-fry sauce ingredients and stir again.

5. Serve with rice.

Instant Pot Egg and Pork Congee

Servings: 2-4 Prep Time: 15 mins Cooking Time: 45 mins

Ingredients

- Salt to taste

- 3 century eggs, cut into 8 – 10 pieces per egg

- 2 thin slices ginger (8 grams)

- 1 pound pork bones

- 1 pound pork shank

- 6 ½ cups cold running tap water

- 1 cup Jasmine rice

Pork seasoning:

- A dash of ground white pepper

- ¼ teaspoon sesame oil

- ½ teaspoon salt

Directions

1. Place rice, pork, bones, ginger and water in the Instant Pot and close the lid. Cook for 35 minutes on high. After the 35 minutes, allow the pressure to release naturally.

2. Remove the bones and pork shank from the pot and shred the pork before seasoning with ground white pepper, ½-teaspoon salt and ¼ teaspoon sesame oil.

3. Press the sauté button and then add the eggs and shredded pork. Season with salt and stir well until you get the desired consistency.

4. Serve, garnish with green onions and enjoy.

Thai Curry

Servings: 4-6 Prep Time: 15 mins Cooking Time: 20 mins

Ingredients

- 2 cups snap peas

- 2 cups cooked quinoa or rice

- 12 ounces broccoli florets

- 1 tablespoon soy sauce (you can add more to taste)

- 1 cup vegetable broth

- 1 can chickpeas, drained and rinsed

- 4 tablespoons green curry paste

- 1 (13.5-ounce) can coconut milk

- 1 can chick peas, drained and rinsed

- ½ inch piece of ginger, peeled and crushed

- 3 cloves garlic, crushed

- 1 medium onion, peeled and thinly sliced

- 1 tablespoon vegetable oil

Garnishes and sides:

- Salt

- Brown sugar

- Sriracha or garlic chili sauce

- Lime wedges

- Basil, minced (preferably Thai basil)

- Cilantro, minced

Directions

1. Press the sauté button on your instant pot and heat the vegetable oil. Add the onion, ginger and garlic and sauté for 3 minutes or until the onion is soft.

2. Add the curry paste and stir. Allow it to cook for 5 minutes before adding in the vegetables and chickpeas. Stir to coat them evenly with the curry and then add the vegetable stock, can of coconut milk and soy sauce. Lock your instant pot and cook for 10 minutes on high.

3. Once ready, allow for quick release. You can add more salt, brown sugar and soy sauce if you wish and sprinkle with basil and cilantro. Serve with the cooked quinoa or rice.

Instant Pot Fish Chowder

Servings: 6 Prep Time: 10 mins Cooking Time: 25 mins

Ingredients

- 1 cup half & half
- 1 cup clam juice
- ½ cup flour
- Salt & pepper to taste
- 1 teaspoon old bay seasoning (or more)
- 2 lbs. cod
- 4 cups organic chicken broth
- 4 cups potatoes, peeled & diced
- ½ cup mushrooms, sliced
- 1 cup onion, chopped
- 2 tablespoons butter
- Optional: 4-6 slices of Bacon

Directions

1. Put trivet inside your Instant Pot and add 1 cup of water.

2. Place the frozen cod on top of the trivet and close the lid. Cook for 9 minutes on manual setting. After the time elapses, release the pressure and then remove the cod and cut it into large chunks. Discard the liquid and put the steel pot inside.

3. Select the sauté option, add the butter, onions and mushrooms, and cook for 2 minutes or until soft. Add chicken broth and potatoes, lock the lid and ensure the valve is closed. Use the manual setting and set time for 8 minutes.

4. After the 8 minutes, release the pressure and season with salt, pepper and Old Bay seasoning and add the fish. Mix the clam juice and flour in a bowl and then pour the mixture into the pot. Turn the pot off and stir in the half-and-half.

5. Serve with buttered rolls.

Pork and Potatoes

Servings: 6-8 Prep Time: 15 mins Cooking Time: 60 mins

Ingredients

- Kosher salt or sea salt, pepper and paprika (to taste)

- 2 tablespoons white wine vinegar

- 1 cup of apple juice

- ½ cup of beef or chicken broth

- 6 potatoes, peeled and cut in half (optional)

- 1 teaspoon of caraway seeds

- 1 teaspoon dry marjoram seasoning

- 1 tablespoon of brown sugar

- 16 ounces of kraut with most of the juice squeezed out

- 1 teaspoon minced garlic

- 1 small onion chopped

- 1 tablespoon of lard or oil

- 2-3 lbs. boneless pork loin roast

Directions

1. Season the pork with salt, paprika and pepper and set aside. Select the sauté option and once the Instant Pot is hot, add the oil or lard and brown the pork on both sides. Once ready, remove the meat and set aside.

2. Add onions and cook until translucent and then add the garlic and continue cooking for 1 more minute. You can add more oil if needed.

3. Add the liquids and use a wooden spoon to scrape the bottom of the Instant Pot. Add kraut, marjoram, brown sugar and caraway seeds and then potatoes and meat on top and close the lid. Click the meat option and set time for 50 minutes,

4. Once ready, allow for natural pressure release followed by a quick release.

5. Serve and enjoy.

Instant Pot Penne and Meatballs

Servings: 4-6 Prep Time: 10 mins Cooking Time: 10 mins

Ingredients

- 48 ounces pasta sauce, divided

- 16-18 ounces penne pasta

- 3 cups water

- 1-2 pounds frozen meatballs

- Parmesan, grated

- 1 tablespoon red pepper flakes, optional

Directions

1. Place the meatballs at the bottom of the Instant Pot and then add 3 cups of water. Place the pasta on top and add half (24 ounces) of pasta sauce and then sprinkle red pepper flakes on top and close the lid. Do not stir the ingredients.

2. Use the manual setting, ensure knob is on the sealing position and adjust time to 6-7 minutes. Once the beep sounds, place knob in venting position and allow for natural pressure release.

3. Stir in the remaining sauce and serve.

Instant Pot Chicken

Servings: 4 Prep Time: 20 mins Cooking Time: 60 mins

Ingredients

- ¼ cup honey

- 3 tablespoons tamari

- ½ teaspoon finely ground black pepper

- ¼ cup ghee

- 2 teaspoons garlic powder

- 1 ½ teaspoons sea salt

- 3 tablespoons ketchup

- 2 pounds boneless chicken thighs

Directions

1. Place the ingredients in the Instant Pot and stir to mix and then close the lid ensuring the valve is in the seal position.

2. Press "manual", and press the "−" option until it displays 18 minutes for fresh chicken or the "+" until 40 minutes is displayed for frozen chicken.

3. After the set cooking time elapses, do a quick release. Remove and shred the chicken. Press cancel and then press the sauté function and let the sauce cook for 5 minutes.

4. Serve with vegetables and rice.

Chicken Carbonara

Servings: 4-6 Prep Time: 10 mins Cooking Time: 20 mins

Ingredients

- 1 cup chicken stock/bone broth

- White wine, splash to deglaze

- Coarsely ground black pepper, to taste

- 1/2 teaspoon salt

- 1 cup parmesan, finely grated

- 3 large eggs, room temperature

- 12 oz. spaghetti/fettuccine, split in half

- 1 medium onion, chopped

- 2 cloves garlic, minced

- 4 slices thick cut bacon, sliced

- 1 lb. chicken breasts, cut into 1 inch cubes

- Fresh parsley (optional)

- Fresh basil (optional)

- Water

Directions

1. Select the sauté function and once hot, add the bacon and cook until browned and crispy. Add onions and stir for 2-3 minutes or until slightly translucent. Add garlic and then a splash of wine to deglaze before adding chicken stock.

2. Cancel the sauté option and add noodles and enough water to cover the noodles and finally add the chicken and close the lid. Ensure valve is on the seal position. Set to manual for 4 minutes. Once the time elapses, allow for natural pressure release.

3. In the meantime, whisk eggs, your favorite herbs, cheese, salt and pepper. Once you open the lid, slowly stir in the mixture. Keep stirring to combine with pasta until it is creamy. Serve.

Brazilian Bean and Meat Stew

Servings: 6-8 Prep Time: 20 mins Cooking Time: 60 mins

Ingredients

- 1 lb. dried black beans, sorted and rinsed

- 1 lb. boneless beef short ribs, cut into 1-inch chunks

- 1 lb. boneless pork shoulder, cut into 1-inch chunks

- 4 ounces diced bacon

- 2 cloves garlic, crushed

- 1 large onion, diced

- 1 lb. smoked sausage

- Fresh parsley, minced (optional)

- Salt and freshly ground black pepper

- 2 bay leaves

- 5 cups water

- 1 teaspoon Kosher salt

- ½ teaspoon salt

- ½ teaspoon baking soda

Directions

1. Press the sauté function and then brown the bacon for 5 minutes or until crispy. Remove the bacon and place it in a large bowl but make sure to leave the fat behind.

2. Season the pork with salt then place it in the instant pot. Brown the pork on both sides, which should take about 3 minutes. Remove the pork (place it in the bowl of bacon).

3. Place the smoked sausage in the instant pot and brown only one side for 2 minutes. Remove the sausage and place it in the bowl with bacon and pork.

4. Place the onion, garlic and ½ teaspoon of salt into the instant pot and cook for at least 5 minutes. Use a wooden spoon to scrape up any meats from the bottom of the instant pot and stir from time to time.

5. Add in the beans, the meats (pork, bacon, sausage) and any juices, baking soda and 1 teaspoon of salt and stir to mix the ingredients. Add the water and bay leaves and lock the lid and cook for 40 minutes on high.

6. Once ready, allow the pressure to release naturally. Remove the lid and discard the bay leaves. Check and adjust the seasoning accordingly. Top up with parsley and serve.

Instant Pot Macaroni and Cheese

Servings: 4 Prep Time: 10 mins Cooking Time: 10 mins

Ingredients

- 1 ½ cups Monterey Jack cheese, shredded

- 1 cup cheddar cheese, shredded

- 12 oz. heavy cream or 1 can evaporated milk

- 4 cups water

- 2 teaspoons kosher salt or 1 teaspoon sea salt

- 1 tablespoon hot pepper sauce

- 2 teaspoons ground yellow mustard

- 2 tablespoons butter

- 1 lb. dried pasta

- 2 tablespoons cream cheese (optional)

Directions

1. Place pasta, hot pepper sauce, butter, mustard, salt and pepper in your Instant Pot and lock the lid. Ensure the pressure valve is closed. Cook for 3 minutes on high.

2. After the 3 minutes, allow for natural pressure release and finally do a quick release.

3. Open the lid and stir in evaporated milk or heavy cream. Press "cancel" and then press the "sauté" option and then proceed to add cheese a little at a time stirring each time until you achieve the desired thickness.

4. Serve and top with crispy bacon if you wish.

Chinese Beef Stew

Servings: 4-6 Prep Time: 10 mins Cooking Time: 35 mins

Ingredients

- 2 lbs. beef round, cubed into one inch pieces

- 1 tablespoon soy sauce

- 2 teaspoons rice wine or sherry

- ½ teaspoon sugar

- 2 medium onions sliced

- 1-2 tablespoons oil

- 1-2 teaspoons corn starch slurry if needed

- 1-2 teaspoons (to taste) fresh ginger chopped finely

- 1 can of mushrooms (optional)

- 1 tablespoon Worcestershire sauce

- ½ cup broth, preferably beef

- Salt and pepper

- 1-2 teaspoons (to taste) garlic powder

- Pinch of smoked paprika

- 2 teaspoons corn starch

Directions

1. Select the sauté function. Wait until it indicates hot before adding the oil and onion. Sauté until onion is translucent and then add the sugar, soy sauce and rice wine. Cook for 30 seconds and then stir in the Worcestershire sauce and beef broth and then close the lid and click on the soup option. This will take 30 minutes.

2. After the 30 minutes, allow the pressure to release. Check the meat to see if it is ready. You can cook for a few more minutes on the stew setting if needed.

3. Add ginger, mushrooms, seasoning and corn-starch to make the soup thicker and cook for 1 more minute if you wish.

4. Serve with vegetables or rice.

Instant Pot Oat Rice with Sausage

Servings: 8 Prep Time: 15 mins Cooking Time: 50 mins

Ingredients

- 1 tablespoon fresh chopped green onion

- 2 tablespoons light soy sauce

- 1 tablespoon dark soy sauce

- 1 tablespoon premium soy sauce

- 1/6 teaspoon chicken broth mix

- 1/8 teaspoon ground white pepper

- 1/3 teaspoon salt

- 1 ½ tablespoon freshly chopped green onion

- 1 tablespoon avocado oil or other cooking oil

- 2 cups cold water

- 1 cup oat rice

- 1 cup long grain rice

- 175g yucca root

- 2 lean Chinese sausages

- 2 tablespoons dried shrimps

Directions

1. Soak the shrimps in cold water beforehand to soften them. Slice the sausages, peel the yucca root and then rinse it before chopping it into small pieces. Rinse both the rice and oat rice and drain.

2. Place avocado oil in your Instant Pot and click the sauté option and adjust to 'more'. Sauté the green onion for a minute and add sausages and shrimp. Stir to combine and cook for 1 minute.

3. Add the oat rice, rice and yucca root and stir and then add the water and the remaining ingredients before closing the lid. Ensure the pressure valve is in the 'scal' position and then click the 'rice' option.

4. Once cooking is done, wait 5 minutes and release the pressure. Serve and garnish with green onions.

Pork Stew with Vegetables

Servings: 6-8 Prep Time: 10 mins Cooking Time: 30 mins

Ingredients

- Cilantro, minced for garnish

- Salt and pepper to taste

- 2 cups corn kernels

- 4 Roma tomatoes, diced

- 6 ounces green beans, cut into 11/2 inch pieces

- 1 small summer squash, diced

- 2 small zucchini, diced

- 1 cup homemade chicken stock

- ½ teaspoon kosher salt

- 1 jalapeno, minced

- 3 cloves garlic, peeled and smashed

- 1 large onion, minced

- 1 tablespoon vegetable oil

- 1 teaspoon kosher salt

- 3 lbs. pork shoulder, cut into 1-inch cubes

Directions

1. Press the sauté option and heat the oil. Season the pork with kosher salt and brown one side only for about 4 minutes. Once the pork is done, set it aside and leave behind as much fat as you can in the Instant Pot.

2. Add onion, jalapeno and garlic and stir to mix before adding ½ teaspoon of salt; cook for 5 minutes or until soft.

3. Add pork plus juices and chicken stock and stir to remove any scrapes from the bottom and then lock the lid. Select manual setting and set for 18 minutes.

4. After the time elapses, do a quick release. Remove the lid and add the vegetables. Lock the lid and set time to 6 minutes on manual setting. Once ready, do a quick release, stir and season.

5. Serve and garnish with radishes, cheese and cilantro.

Instant Pot Acini Di Pepe Beef Soup

Servings: 4 Prep Time: 15 mins Cooking Time: 50 mins

Ingredients

- Grated parmesan cheese, optional

- 4 oz. small pasta such as Acini di pepe

- 2 bay leaves

- 32 oz. beef stock

- 28 oz. can diced tomatoes

- ½ cup diced carrot

- ½ cup diced celery

- ½ cup diced onion

    o ½ teaspoon kosher salt

- 1 lb. 90% lean ground beef

Directions

1. Press the sauté function. Once the Instant Pot is hot, add beef, season it with salt and brown it. Use a wooden spoon to break it up as it browns. Add onion, carrots, celery, and sauté for 3-4 more minutes.

2. Add tomatoes, bay leaf, beef stock, close the lid, and then select the soup option. This will set cooking time to 35 minutes.

3. Once ready, do a quick release. Open the lid, stir in the pasta and cover the lid. Use the manual setting and set time for 6 minutes. Release pressure.

4. Remove the bay leaves before serving.

Chicken Marsala

Servings: 4-6 Prep Time: 10 mins Cooking Time: 25 mins

Ingredients

- 2 cups spinach

- 2 tablespoons flour

- 2 tablespoons butter

- Freshly ground black pepper to taste

- 1 teaspoon salt

- ½ cup marsala wine, dry

- 2 cups chicken stock

- 1 teaspoon fresh thyme

- 2 sprigs fresh rosemary

- 8 oz. baby Portobello mushrooms, sliced

- 1 garlic clove, minced

- 1 cup onion, diced

- 1 tablespoon olive oil

- Salt and pepper

- 2 lbs. boneless, skinless chicken thighs

- Freshly grated parmesan cheese for garnish

- 1 lb. linguini, cooked per package directions

Directions

1. Press the sauté function and add the olive oil once the Instant Pot is hot. Use salt and pepper to season the chicken and then brown it on both sides. Remove from the pot and set aside.

2. Add onion and sauté and then add garlic, thyme, rosemary, mushrooms, chicken stock, salt, pepper and wine, put the chicken on top and lock the lid. Ensure that the steam release valve is closed. Click warm/cancel and use the manual setting to adjust time to 10 minutes.

3. In the meantime, melt the butter in a pan, add the flour and cook for 2 minutes stirring occasionally. Remove and set aside.

4. Once the Instant Pot beeps, allow for natural pressure release and remove the chicken. Click the sauté function; add the butter mixture to the pot to thicken the liquid. Add the pasta and spinach and stir.

5. Serve and garnish with parmesan.

Instant Pot Picadillo

Servings: 6 Prep Time: 10 mins Cooking Time: 20 mins

Ingredients

- 1 ½ lb. lean ground beef
- 2 tablespoons capers
- 1 bay leaf
- 1 teaspoon ground cumin
- 4 oz. can tomato sauce
- 2 tablespoons cilantro
- ½ red bell pepper, finely chopped
- 1 teaspoon kosher salt
- 1 tomato, chopped
- 2 cloves garlic, minced
- ½ onion, chopped

Directions

1. Click the sauté option and once hot brown the meat. You can use a wooden spoon to break up the meat as you brown. Add the onion, tomato, garlic, cilantro, salt and pepper and cook for 1 more minute stirring from time to time.

2. Add capers, bay leaf, cumin, water, tomato sauce and stir to mix. Lock the lid in place and cook for 15 minutes on high.

3. Allow for natural pressure release or do a quick release. Serve the chicken with vegetables and enjoy.

Instant Pot Keema

Servings: 4 Prep Time: 15 mins Cooking Time: 50 mins

Ingredients

- 2 cups peas

- 1 (14.5 ounce) can diced tomatoes

- 1 pound ground beef or lamb

- ¼ teaspoon ground cardamom

- ¼ teaspoon cayenne

- ½ teaspoon cumin powder

- ½ teaspoon garam masala

- ½ teaspoon black pepper

- ½ teaspoon turmeric

- 1 teaspoon salt

- 1 teaspoon paprika

- 1 tablespoon coriander powder

- 1 Serrano pepper, minced

- 1-inch fresh ginger, minced

- 4 cloves garlic, minced

- 1 onion, finely diced

- 2 tablespoons ghee

- Cilantro, optional for garnish

Directions

1. Select the sauté function and add the ghee and onions. Sauté until the onion begins to brown.

2. Add garlic, ginger, spices and Serrano pepper and cook for 30 seconds before adding the beef. Cook the beef until mostly browned and then stir in the peas and tomatoes. Close the lid, cancel the keep warm function and click the bean/chili option. This will set the time for 30 minutes.

3. Once ready, allow for natural pressure release before opening the lid. If there is extra liquid, you can sauté for 10-15 minutes.

4. Serve and garnish with cilantro.

Instant Pot Vegetable Pulao

Servings: 4-6 Prep Time: 10 mins Cooking Time: 20 mins

Ingredients

- 2 tablespoons vegetable oil

- 10-15 raw cashew nuts, chopped or split in half (optional)

- Salt to taste

- 1-2 Green chilies, halved

- ¾ tablespoon freshly ground ginger garlic paste

- 1/3 tablespoon freshly ground garam masala powder

- ¼ cup chopped fresh mint leaves (or 1/8 cup dried mint leaves)

- 1/3 teaspoon turmeric powder

- ½ medium size onion, thinly sliced

- 1 medium potato, cubed

- 4 cups chopped mixed vegetables (carrots, Green peas and string beans)

- 2 cups Basmati rice

- *Whole Garam Masala:*

- 1 bay leaf

- 3 cardamom

- 3 cloves

- 3-inch long cinnamon stick

- 1/3 tablespoon caraway seeds (optional)

Directions

1. Select the sauté function and add oil when the Instant Pot is hot. Add caraway seeds, cloves, cinnamon, bay leaf and cardamom and stir to mix. Add the cashew nuts and cook for a few seconds, then add the onions and cook until translucent.

2. Add ginger-garlic paste, turmeric powder and green chiles and cook for some minutes before adding the vegetables except the potatoes. Cook for 1 more minute. Add potatoes and sauté for another minute. Add mint leaves, masala powder, 3 cups of water and salt. Stir and then add the rice and stir to mix.

3. Cancel the sauté function and close the lid. Put the sealing in place and click the rice button. This will set time for 12 minutes on low. Once the cooking is done, allow the pressure to release naturally.

4. Open the lid, fluff the rice and serve.

Curried Potatoes

Servings: 4 Prep Time: 5 mins Cooking Time: 10 mins

Ingredients

- ½ teaspoon salt

- ¼ teaspoon ginger

- 1 teaspoon coriander

- 1 teaspoon turmeric

- 1 cup crushed or diced tomatoes

- 2 potatoes, peeled & cubed

- ½ tablespoon cumin seeds, whole

- 1 large onion, chopped

- Optional: 1 cup cooked garbanzo beans

Directions

1. Place ½ cup of water in your Instant pot. Add the onions and cumin seeds and cook for 2-3 minutes before adding the potatoes, turmeric, tomatoes, ginger, coriander, salt and ¼ cup water and then lock the lid. Cook on manual high for 5 minutes.

2. After the 5 minutes, do a quick release. Serve the potatoes with brown rice.

Pasta Fagioli

Servings: 8 Prep Time: 15 mins Cooking Time: 30 mins

Ingredients

- 3 tablespoons nutritional yeast
- 10 ounces kale, stems removed and leaves chopped
- 2 cups whole grain small pasta
- 2 teaspoons salt
- ½ teaspoon smoked paprika
- 2 teaspoons dried oregano, divided
- 3 teaspoons dried basil leaves, divided
- 26 ounces chopped tomatoes, canned
- ¼ teaspoon red pepper flakes
- 1 teaspoon fresh rosemary, minced
- 7 cloves garlic, minced and divided

- 2 ribs celery, chopped

- 1 medium onion, chopped

- 2 cups dried cranberry beans

- Freshly ground black pepper, to taste

Directions

1. Sort the beans and soak them in water overnight, drain and rinse.

2. Select the sauté function and once it is hot, add onion and a few tablespoons of water. You can add a pinch of baking soda if you wish and then add red pepper flakes, ½ the garlic, celery, rosemary and sauté for 2 more minutes.

3. Add the tomatoes, basil, paprika and oregano and stir for a few minutes before adding the water or vegetable broth and beans and locking the lid.

4. Set time for 10 minutes on high. After the 10 minutes elapse, allow for natural pressure release and then do a quick release.

5. Open the lid and add remaining garlic, oregano, basil, adjust the seasoning and then add the pasta and click the sauté function. Stir from time to time and then add the kale and cook for about 5 minutes or until it wilts.

6. Serve and enjoy.

Instant Pot Soup

Servings: 4 Prep Time: 10 mins Cooking Time: 25 mins

Ingredients

- 1 cup milk or cream

- 1 pound hot Italian sausage

- 32 oz. low sodium chicken broth

- 2 cups diced Potatoes

- 2 cups chopped Kale

- 3 cloves garlic

- 1 tablespoon olive oil

- 1 small chopped onion

- 6 slices cooked bacon

Directions

1. Press the sauté option and add olive oil once the Instant pot is hot. Add garlic, onions, sausage, and sauté until sausage browns and crumbles.

2. Add potatoes and chicken broth and then put the kale on top and cover the lid. Use the manual setting and set time for 15 minutes on high.

3. Do a quick release and click sauté. Stir in the milk or cream and chopped bacon.

4. Serve with Italian bread.

Chicken Chili

Servings: 4 Prep Time: 10 mins Cooking Time: 15 mins

Ingredients

- 1 cup bacon, cooked and diced
- 14 ounces whole kernel corn, canned
- 10 ounces diced tomatoes with green chiles
- 2 cups chicken broth/stock
- 1 teaspoon oregano, dried
- ¼ teaspoon black pepper
- ⅛ teaspoon salt
- 1 teaspoon cumin
- 2 teaspoons chili powder
- 3 ⅓ cups cooked and diced boneless chicken breasts
- 3 teaspoons minced garlic cloves
- ⅔ cup seeded and diced jalapeño
- 1 ¼ cups diced onion

Directions

1. Place chicken, chicken broth, onions, jalapeno, garlic, chili powder, oregano, cumin, salt, black pepper, tomatoes and corn in your Instant Pot and lock the lid. Ensure steam nozzle is sealed and then select the soup setting and adjust the time to 10 minutes.

2. Release the pressure and set on warm. Stir in the cheese and ½ the bacon and let it cook for 3 minutes.

3. Serve with remaining bacon and garnish with cheese.

Instant Pot Italian Chicken

Servings: 6-8 Prep Time: 15 mins Cooking Time: 50 mins

Ingredients

- ¾ cup mushrooms, thinly sliced

- 2 lbs. chicken breasts

- 2 tablespoons pesto

- ¾ cup marinara

- ¼ teaspoon salt

- ½ cup red bell pepper

- ½ cup green bell pepper

- ¾ cup onion

- 1 tablespoon olive oil

Directions

1. Press the sauté option and once it says hot, add the oil. Add onion and bell peppers and season with salt and then cook for 3-4 minutes before adding the chicken, pesto and marinara. Set the time for 12 minutes on high for thawed chicken and 20 minutes for frozen chicken.

2. Once the set time elapses, remove the chicken breasts and shred and then remove 2/3 cup of liquid. Do not remove the vegetables. You can use the liquid you removed to make rice or soup if you wish.

3. Add the mushrooms to the Instant pot and cook for another 2-3 minutes on the sauté setting. Place the shredded chicken in the Instant pot and stir to combine.

4. Serve over rice and enjoy.

Thai Peanut Chicken

Servings: 6-8 Prep Time: 15 mins Cooking Time: 40 mins

Ingredients

- 2 lbs. chicken breasts

- 1 cup Thai peanut sauce

- ½ red bell pepper

- ½ onion

- 1 tablespoon olive oil

Directions

1. Select the sauté function and once hot, add oil and then add onions and bell peppers and cook for 3-4 minutes.

2. Add chicken and Thai peanut sauce and close the lid; if chicken is thawed, set time for 12 minutes on high but if it is frozen set time for 20 minutes on high.

3. After the set time, release the pressure, remove the chicken and shred. If you are going to cook rice, you can remove 2/3 cup of liquid from the pot to cook it in.

4. Return the shredded chicken to your Instant Pot and mix with the remaining liquid.

5. Serve the chicken over rice and vegetables and enjoy.

Instant Pot Cranberry beans

Servings: 7 Prep Time: 10 mins Cooking Time: 45 mins

Ingredients

- 1 ½ teaspoons sea salt
- 1 teaspoon dried oregano
- 1 tablespoon chili powder
- 1 ½ teaspoons cumin
- 1/3 cup chopped cilantro leaves
- 4 garlic cloves, peeled and minced
- 1 onion, peeled and chopped
- 3 ¼ cups water
- 1 lb. dried cranberry beans soaked
- Cooked rice (optional)

Directions

1. Sort the beans and soak them for at least 6 hours, drain and rinse.

2. Place the beans in your Instant Pot and add the water. Make sure the beans are covered with water. You can add a bit more water if needed. Add onion and garlic and lock the lid. Ensure the knob is turned to 'sealing' and then press on the bean/chilli option. Set the time to 45 minutes.

3. Once ready, let the pressure release naturally. Add the remaining ingredients, stir and let it rest for a few minutes.

4. Serve with rice and vegetables and garnish with cilantro.

Chili Macaroni

Servings: 6-8 Prep Time: 10 mins Cooking Time: 15 mins

Ingredients

- A big handful of chopped spinach
- 3 ½ cups water
- 1 (1 lb.) package macaroni
- 1 cup frozen corn
- ½ green pepper, diced
- ½ red pepper, diced
- 1 carrot, peeled and diced
- 2 cups cooked or 1 can beans, drained and rinsed
- 1 (28 oz.) can diced tomatoes
- 1 (14 oz.) can plain tomato sauce
- 2 cloves garlic, minced
- 1 small yellow onion, diced
- 1 Tablespoon dried oregano

- 2 tablespoons chili powder blend
- ½ teaspoon garlic powder
- ½ teaspoon onion powder
- 1 teaspoon smoked paprika
- 1 teaspoon ground coriander
- 1 teaspoon ground cumin
- 2 teaspoons Ancho chili powder
- 1 tablespoon dried oregano

Directions

1. Press the sauté function and wait for the Instant Pot to become hot. Add a bit of water, onions and sauté until the onions are translucent before adding the garlic and cooking for 1 more minute.

2. Add spices and oregano and stir to mix. Add tomatoes, sauce, stir and wait for it to simmer and then cancel the sauté function.

3. Add the beans and vegetables, stir and then place the macaroni on top without stirring. Add remaining water and close the lid. Ensure pressure release valve is set to 'sealing'. Use the manual setting and adjust time to 4 minutes on low.

4. After the 4 minutes elapse, do a quick release. Open and stir in the spinach until it wilts.

5. Serve and sprinkle parmesan cheese on top.

Chinese Congee

Servings: 6 Prep Time: 10 mins Cooking Time: 40 mins

Ingredients

- 1 tablespoon oats

- 1 tablespoon quinoa

- 2 (200g) eddo

- 200g yum, peeled, rinsed and cubed

- 3-4 Chinese dates

- 1 tablespoon crushed corn

- 1 tablespoon dry black eye beans

- 1 tablespoon dry mung beans

- 1 tablespoon dry lotus seeds

- 1 tablespoon red beans

- 1 tablespoon dry Lily

- 2 tablespoons brown rice

- 1 ½ tablespoons buckwheat

- 1 tablespoon millet

- 1 tablespoon pearl barley

- 1 tablespoon Gordon Euryale seeds

- 1 ½ tablespoons Romano beans

Directions

1. Soak beans and Gordon Euryale seeds in the morning.

2. Place all the ingredients in your Instant pot, add 5 cups of water and lock the lid. Ensure valve is in the seal position. Press manual setting and set time for 30 minutes.

3. Once ready, wait 10 minutes and release the pressure slowly. Serve & enjoy.

Snacks, Desserts and Appetizers

Azuki Bean Soup

Servings: 6 Prep Time: 5 mins Cooking Time: 5 mins

Ingredients

- 8-12 cups of water (for thick or thinner soup)

- 4 tablespoons of sugar (you can use more or less according to your preference)

- 2 small pieces of lemon peel, broken into tiny pieces (optional)

- ½ cup of dry chestnuts (optional)

- ½ cup of dry lotus seeds, with the sprouts removed

- 2 cups of red beans

Directions

1. Place the ingredients in your Instant pot and click the bean/chilli function. Press adjust once. This will extend the cooking time.

2. Once cooking is done, stir before serving.

Steamed Corns

Servings: 6 Prep Time: 5 mins Cooking Time: 10 mins

Ingredients

- 6 fresh young corns

Directions

1. Remove husk and rinse the corns with water.

2. Place the steam rack in your Instant pot, add 2 cups of water and then place the corns inside; you can stack them on top of each other.

3. Cover the lid and ensure the valve is sealed. Select the steam option and set time for 12 minutes.

4. Once cooking is done, wait for 5 minutes and then release the pressure.

5. Serve and enjoy.

Thai Carrot Soup

Servings: 6 Prep Time: 5 mins Cooking Time: 15 mins

Ingredients

- ½ cup cream or full fat coconut milk
- Cilantro, chopped
- ¼ teaspoon turmeric
- ¼ teaspoon garam masala
- ½ teaspoon curry powder
- 1 teaspoon garlic powder
- 1 teaspoon sea salt or 1 tablespoon fish sauce
- 4 cups broth, veggie or chicken
- 2 teaspoons grated ginger
- 1 jalapeno or Serrano pepper, with seeds, roughly chopped (remove seeds if you prefer a milder taste)
- 1 ¼ lb. carrot, roughly chopped

- 1 medium yellow onion, roughly chopped

- 1 tablespoon avocado oil or other fat

- 20 drops stevia or 3 tablespoons honey (optional)

- ¼ teaspoon cayenne pepper (optional)

Directions

1. Press the sauté function, add the oil and sauté onions for 3-5 minutes. Add carrot and pepper, and cook for a few more minutes, and then add the broth and spices. Stir and lock the lid. Use the manual setting to set time for 12 minutes.

2. Once time is up, do a quick release. Remove the lid, stir in cilantro and then puree the soup. You can use an immersion blender or food processor.

3. Return to pot and add cream or stevia if you wish. Serve.

Instant Pot Popcorn

Servings: 4-6 Prep Time: 2 mins Cooking Time: 3 mins

Ingredients

- ½ cup popcorn kernels

- 2 tablespoons of butter

- 3 tablespoons of coconut oil

Directions

1. Press sauté and then press adjust in order to increase the temperature to more. Once the display indicates hot, add the coconut oil.

2. After 1 minute, spread corn kernels inside the pot, stir to mix with butter and cover the pot. The kernels will start popping after about 2 minutes. Turn off your instant pot once two thirds of the kernels have popped and let it sit to pop the rest.

3. Open the lid, season and serve.

Instant Pot Potato Salad

Servings: 4 Prep Time: 5 mins Cooking Time: 5 mins

Ingredients

- Salt and pepper taste

- 6 drops dill essential oil

- 1 tablespoon parsley

- 1 tablespoon ground mustard

- 2 tablespoons dill pickle juice

- 1 cup mayonnaise

- ¼ cup chopped onion

- 1 ½ cups water

- 4 eggs

- 5-6 medium russet potatoes, peeled and cubed

Directions

1. Place the steamer basket inside your Instant pot and then add water, potatoes and eggs. Lock the lid and use

the manual setting to set the time for 4 minutes on high. Once time is up, do a quick release.

2. Place eggs in cold water and then peel and dice. Place potatoes in a dish along with dressing ingredients and mix. Add the eggs, salt, pepper, parsley and mix to combine.

3. Put in the fridge for 1 hour and serve.

Instant Pot Lemon Cheesecake

Servings: 6 Prep Time: 20 mins Cooking Time: 25 mins

Ingredients

- 1 ½ cups water

- 1 jar lemon curd

- 3 eggs, at room temperature

- Zest of one lemon

- 1 tablespoon lemon juice

- ¼ cup sour cream, at room temperature

- ½ teaspoon vanilla

- 1 teaspoon flour

- ½ cup sugar

- 16 oz cream cheese, at room temperature

- Raspberries (optional)

- 6 half pint mason jars

Directions

1. In a bowl, whisk together flour, cream cheese and sugar until smooth. Add sour cream, lemon juice, vanilla and lemon zest and mix well before adding one egg at a time.

2. Fill the 6 jars with ¼ cup of cheesecake each and then add 1 tablespoon of lemon curd in each of the jars and then add another ¼ cup of cheesecake batter in each jar before covering the jars with foil.

3. Place the trivet in your Instant pot and add 1 ½ cups of water. Place 3 jars on the trivet and then stuck the rest on top of the other 3 jars. Lock the lid and ensure the vent is sealed. Use the manual setting and set time for 8 minutes on high.

4. When cooking is done, allow for natural pressure release for at least 15 minutes. Remove jars using a towel or gloves. Let the jars cool.

5. Serve and garnish with raspberries.

Instant Pot Chocolate Cake

Servings: 4 Prep Time: 15 mins Cooking Time: 45 mins

Ingredients

- Frosting of your choice

- 1 cup chocolate chips

- 1 Boxed cake mix (15.25 oz.)

Directions

1. Start by preparing the cake mix according to the box's directions. Add the chocolate chips then divide the batter between 2 bowls.

2. Spray a 7-inch spring form pan with non-stick spray and then pour half of the batter into the pan before covering the pan loosely with a foil.

3. Place the trivet inside the pot then add 1 cup of water and then use a foil sling to place the cake on the trivet. Close the lid and ensure the vent is sealed. Use the manual setting and set time for 30 minutes on high.

4. Once cooking is done, allow for pressure to release naturally for around 15 minutes.

5. Remove cake and let it rest on a wire rack for about 10 minutes and then remove from pan. Cook the remaining batter by repeating the process.

6. You can frost cake as you wish before serving.

Lemon Curd

Servings: 2 Prep Time: 5 mins Cooking Time: 30 mins

Ingredients

- 3 large eggs and 1 yolk

- 1 teaspoon grated lemon peel

- ¾ cup fresh lemon juice

- 1 1/3 cup of sugar

- ¼ cup of melted butter (half stick)

Directions

1. In a bowl, mix together butter and sugar and then stir in the eggs, yolk, and lemon peel and lemon juice. Pour the mixture into jars but ensure you don't fully fill the jars and then close the jars.

2. Place trivet or steam basket into your Instant pot and add 2 cups of water and then place jars on top. Close the lid and ensure the vent is closed. Use the manual setting and set time to 9 minutes on high.

3. Once time is up, allow for natural pressure release for 10 minutes. Remove jars, open and stir and close the lids again. Wait for 20 minutes then refrigerate for 4 hours. You can place them in the fridge after 10 minutes.

4. Serve on scones or cakes.

Tapioca Pudding

Servings: 8-12 Prep Time: 10 mins Cooking Time: 30 mins

Ingredients

- 1 tablespoon vanilla

- 2 egg yolks

- 1 can coconut milk

- 1/4 cup raw honey (or more if you prefer sweeter)

- 1/2 teaspoon sea salt

- 3 cups water

- 1 cup tapioca pearls (not instant)

Directions

1. Place water and tapioca pearls inside the Instant pot. Using the manual setting, set time to 6 minutes.

2. Once cooking is done, allow for natural pressure release (for around 20 minutes), release any remaining pressure and then remove the lid.

3. Then add honey and salt and stir to mix.

4. In small bowl, whisk together egg yolks and coconut milk and then place them in the Instant Pot. Press on the sauté function and then cook until it boils. Turn the heat off then add vanilla and stir.

5. Remove and serve with diced fruit if you wish.

Caramel Pot de Creme

Servings: 4 Prep Time: 15 mins Cooking Time: 35 mins

Ingredients

- Sea salt, optional

- ½ teaspoon vanilla extract

- 1 cup heavy whipping cream

- ¼ cup water

- 1/3 cup granulated sugar

- 3 large egg yolks

Directions

1. In a bowl, whisk egg yolks and then set aside. Mix together sugar and water and boil in a saucepan over medium-high heat until the mixture turns brown but not burned.

2. Lower heat to medium low and then slowly add the cream slowly ensuring to whisk it until the caramel bits dissolve.

3. Mix together 1 tablespoon of cream mixture and egg yolks then add vanilla and stir. Divide the mixture equally between 4 ramekins or mason jars.

4. Place trivet into your Instant pot and add 1 1/2 cups of water. Place the ramekins on top of the trivet. Use manual setting and set time to 6 minutes. Ensure knob is in the sealed, not vent, position.

5. Once cooking is done, allow for natural pressure release (around 20 minutes).

6. Remove the ramekins and refrigerate for at least 4 hours before serving.

Dulce de Leche

Servings: 12 Prep Time: 10 mins Cooking Time: 60 mins

Ingredients

- Water

- 2 (8 ounce) canning jars with lid and ring

- 1 (14 ounce) can sweetened condensed milk

Directions

1. Divide condensed milk in two parts then put the parts into each of the 2 ounce canning jars, then close the jars tightly with rings and lids.

2. Put the stainless steel rack inside your Instant pot (the jars should not touch the instant pot directly) and put the two jars on top.

3. Add enough water so that it reaches half way up the jars and then lock the lid. Use the manual setting and set time to 30 minutes. You can increase time to 45 minutes

if you wish for a darker, thicker dulce de leche. Ensure knob is set to sealing, not venting.

4. Once cooking is complete, allow for natural pressure release (give it 15minutes).

5. Remove the jars using oven mitts and let them cool for at least 15 minutes.

6. Open the lids, stir well and serve. You can store any leftovers up to a couple of weeks in the fridge.

Egg Muffins

Servings: 4 Prep Time: 10 mins Cooking Time: 15 mins

Ingredients

- 4 slices precooked bacon, crumbled

- 1 green onion, diced

- 4 tablespoons shredded cheddar/Jack cheese

- ¼ teaspoon lemon pepper seasoning

- 4 eggs

Directions

1. Place a steamer basket inside your Instant pot and add 1 1/2 cups of water.

2. Then break the 4 eggs into a measuring bowl that has a pour spout before adding lemon pepper. Beat everything well.

3. Divide the green onion, bacon and cheese evenly between 4 muffin cups. Then pour the eggs you've

beaten into each muffin cup and then stir well with a fork until nicely combined.

4. Then gently place the muffin cups on the steamer basket, cover it nicely and then lock the lid. Cook for 8 minutes on high pressure.

5. Once cooking is done, wait for 2 minutes and then do a quick release.

6. Remove and serve.

Mexican-Inspired Corn On The Cob

Servings: 4 Prep Time: 5 mins Cooking Time: 15 mins

Ingredients

- 1 tablespoon fresh lime juice

- 1/4 teaspoon salt (or to taste)

- 1/4 teaspoon cayenne pepper (or to taste)

- 1 small clove garlic, peeled

- 2 tablespoons nutritional yeast

- 2 tablespoons hemp hearts (you can use sesame seeds or sunflower seeds if you wish)

- 1/2 cup plain, unsweetened almond milk (or any other non-dairy milk)

- 1 tablespoon brown rice flour

- 4 ears corn, shucked and rinsed

- *Garnishes:*

- Jalapeno or other hot peppers

- Lime wedges, and/or chipotle powder/smoked paprika

- Minced cilantro or parsley, chopped

Directions

1. Start by cooking the corn in whichever method you want to use (you can use the instant pot to cook). To cook with an Instant Pot, place the steaming basket or rack inside your Instant pot before placing the corn on the rack. Then add about 1 ½ cups of water (enough to cover the bottom by at least ½ inch but not too much to rise above the bottom of the rack) and then cook for about 4 minutes of high.

2. Once cooking is complete, do a quick release.

3. In the meantime, make the 'sauce' by mixing together the remaining ingredients minus the lime juice and garnishes in a blender then blend the ingredients until smooth. You can then cook over medium heat ensuring to stir constantly until it thickens and boils.

4. Then you can add lime juice and then continue cooking for a minute or two. But if the sauce is too thick to pour or drizzle, try adding some more non-dairy milk (use a tablespoon) to thin it out. Then taste before adding some more lime juice, cayenne and salt if you want. Then remove from heat and serve the corn with drizzled hot sauce then sprinkle with your preferred garnishes.

5. Serve the corn drizzled with the hot sauce and sprinkled with your choice of garnishes.

Instant Pot Magic Cake

Servings: 4 Prep Time: 15 mins Cooking Time: 50 mins

Ingredients

- Powdered sugar for dusting

- 2 cups lukewarm milk

- 1 stick melted butter

- 1 TSP Vanilla

- 3/4 cup flour

- 3/4 cup sugar

- 4 eggs

Directions

1. Separate the eggs then mix the egg whites with a mixer until you have stiff peaks.

2. Next, beat the egg yolks using sugar until it is nicely blended before melting the butter then add in the

vanilla. Continue to mix with the mixer then start slowly to add in the flour until it is mixed fully in.

3. Then add milk slowly and continue adding that until it is completely incorporated. After that, you can add the egg whites, about a third at a time then fold into the batter. Make sure to repeat the process until you have folded all the egg whites in.

4. Once the batter is ready, place it in a 7-inch springform pan.

5. Then pour 1 cup of water into the instant pot and place trivet inside.

6. Use a foil to make a sling then lower onto the trivet before covering the pot loosely with foil.

7. Use the manual setting and set time for 40 minutes on high.

8. Once time is up, do a quick release. Remove cake and let it cool before sprinkling with powdered sugar.

9. Serve and enjoy.

Instant Pot Applesauce

Servings: 3 cups Prep Time: 10 mins Cooking Time: 25 mins

Ingredients

- 1 cup filtered water

- 1/4 teaspoon Celtic sea salt

- Juice of 1/2 organic lemon

- 1 tablespoon light colored raw honey

- 1 tablespoon ground cinnamon

- 2 tablespoons pasture butter or ghee

- 12 organic apples, peeled if preferred and quartered

Directions

1. Start by washing and preparing the apples then quarter them and then add the apples, butter, honey, sea salt, cinnamon and water into your Instant pot and lock the lid. Ensure the vent is sealed. Then press the manual button to turn the high pressure light on (red). You can

switch the manual again to move it from low pressure to high pressure. Use the "-" to lower the time to 3.

2. Once the beep sounds after the Instant Pot is done cooking, you can press the 'Keep warm/cancel' button before unplugging the Instant pot. Allow for natural pressure release, around 15 minutes.

3. After the silver circle next to the vent goes down, open the lid and remove the contents. Place the apples in a food processor (you can use half of the liquid in your Instant Pot) and pulse until smooth and fully combined. You can add more liquid if needed.

4. Serve warm or cold.

Beef Barley Soup

Servings: 6-8 Prep Time: 20 mins Cooking Time: 1 hr 30 mins

Ingredients

- 2/3 cup pearl barley, rinsed

- 1 large potato, shredded (using a food processor or grater)

- ½ teaspoon dried thyme

- 2 bay leaves

- 1 cup water

- 6 cups low sodium beef broth (or vegetable)

- 6-8 cloves garlic, minced

- 3 cups mirepoix (a mixture of chopped carrots, celery and onion)

- 2 tablespoons oil

- 10 baby bella mushrooms, quartered

- Salt and pepper

- 1 ½ pounds stew meat

Directions

1. Start by seasoning the stew meat with the pepper and salt. Then proceed to heat 1 tablespoon of oil over medium heat in the instant pot.

2. Next, add about ½ of the stew meat and then brown it on all sides, for about 2-3 minutes before removing the meat to a plate.

3. Once done, repeat these steps for the second batch as well as the second tablespoon of oil.

4. Then add the mushrooms to the pot then brown them until they start to pick up brown bits that were left behind by the meat, for about 1-2 minutes. Once done, remove the mushroom from the heat to the same plate as the stew meat.

5. Once done, you can add a little oil to the pot as well as the mirepoix mix (if necessary). Then proceed to cook the veggies until the onions are translucent and soft, for about 4-5 minutes, before adding the garlic then cook for another 30 seconds.

6. Then you can add the beef broth, water, dried thyme, bay leaves, mushrooms and the stew meat in the instant

pot before covering. Then cook pressure cook for about 13-16 minutes, depending on how big the meat is.

7. Once you do all that, let the pressure to release before you remove the lid.

8. Then add in the shredded potatoes as well as the barley then let the soup to cook for about 1 hour (on the high setting- just hit the slow cook button) or until the barley and the potatoes cook through. You can then season with salt and pepper before serving with chopped parsley on top as well as crackers or a loaf of crusty bread.

Steamed Crab Legs

Servings: 4 Prep Time: 2 mins Cooking Time: 2 mins

Ingredients

- Lemon juice

- 4 tablespoons butter, melted

- ¾ cup water

- 2 lbs frozen crab legs

Directions

1. Place the steamer basket in your Instant pot and arrange crab legs on top. Add the water and close the lid and valve. Cook for 2 minutes on high (until they are bright pink). Once cooking is done, do a quick release.

2. Stir in melted butter and serve.

Instant Pot Tomato Soup

Servings: 4 Prep Time: 10 mins Cooking Time: 25 mins

Ingredients

- ¼ cup sugar

- 1 tablespoon balsamic vinegar

- Salt and pepper, to taste

- 1 tablespoon dried basil

- 2 teaspoons dried parsley

- 3 cups chicken stock

- 2 28-ounce cans whole tomatoes

- 2 tablespoons tomato paste

- 1 tablespoon oil

- 1 medium onion, diced

1. Activate your instant pot's sauté function and allow the pot to heat up. Add oil and sauté onion and tomato paste for about 3 minutes. And then turn off the pot. Add tomatoes and any tomato juices then the stock and stir and then add basil, parsley, salt and pepper. Close the lid and ensure the valve is closed before pressing on the soup setting. Adjust time to 10 minutes.

2. Once cooking is done, let it rest for 10 minutes and then release the pressure.

3. Open the lid and stir in the balsamic vinegar and sugar. You can use an immersion blender to puree then place. Add seasoning if needed and serve immediately.

Chocolate Cheesecake

Servings: 12 Prep Time: 15 mins Cooking Time: 25 mins

Ingredients

- ½ cup sour cream
- 1 tablespoon vanilla
- ¼ cup sugar free Coco powder
- ½ cup Splenda or swerve
- 4 eggs (room temp)
- 4 eight ounce blocks cream cheese (room temp)

Directions

1. Blend all the ingredients until smooth.

2. Pour all the ingredients into a greased 7-inch spring form pan. You can use a spatula to spread the mixture evenly. Place the pan in the instant pot then cook on high for 25 minutes or 15 minutes on natural release.

3. Remove and allow the cheesecake to cool for at least 3 hours in the fridge before serving.

Bread Pudding

Servings: 6 Prep Time: 10 mins Cooking Time: 40 mins

Ingredients

- ½ - ¾ cup sugar

- ½ teaspoon salt

- 1 teaspoon vanilla

- 3 cups milk

- 3 eggs

- 6 slices raisin bread, cut up

Directions

1. In a mixing bowl, mix all the ingredients except the bread. Once well mixed, put bread in a bowl and pour the custard over the bread. Let this sit for around 15 minutes to allow the bread to absorb the egg mixture.

Put a tablespoon of butter on top and cover slightly with aluminum foil.

2. Put a trivet in the inner pot of your instant pot and add two cups of water. Lower the bowl into the instant pot and lock lid in place.

3. Use manual setting on high and set the timer for 25 minutes. After the time elapses, allow quick release, and then remove the pot from the instant pot.

4. You can serve the pudding right away or put in the fridge and serve cold.

Instant Pot Pumpkin Pie

Servings: 6-8 Prep Time: 15 mins Cooking Time: 50 mins

Ingredients

Crust:

- 2 tablespoons melted butter

- 1/3 cup chopped toasted pecans

- ½ cup crushed pecan cookies

Filling:

- ½ cup evaporated milk

- 1 ½ cups solid pack pumpkin

- 1 egg, beaten

- 1 ½ teaspoons pumpkin pie spice

- ½ teaspoon salt

- ½ cup light brown sugar

Directions

1. Coat a 7-inch spring form pan with non-stick cooking spray.

2. Combine butter, pecans and cookie crumbs in a bowl and then spread this in the bottom of the prepared pan. Put this in the freezer for 10 minutes.

3. To prepare the filling, combine pumpkin pie spice, salt and sugar. Whisk in the egg, evaporated milk and pumpkin. Once well combined, pour this into the piecrust and cover the pan with aluminum foil.

4. Pour 1 cup of water into the instant pot then place a trivet at the bottom. Center the pan carefully on the trivet, lock lid and use manual setting to cook at high pressure for around 30 minutes.

5. Once the time elapses, use natural pressure release for around 10 minutes and then do quick release to remove any remaining pressure.

6. Remove the pie and check if set. If it is not set, cook for another 5 minutes. Once ready, transfer the pan to a wire rack and allow to cool. Remove the foil once cooled and refrigerate for a few hours.

7. Serve with whipped cream.

Conclusion

Thank you again for choosing this book!

I hope you have now learned how to prepare many different recipes in your instant pot. You now have no reason for that instant pot to sit in your kitchen cabinet without being used.

Finally, if you enjoyed this book, would you be kind enough to leave a review for this book on Amazon?

Thank you and good luck!

CPSIA information can be obtained
at www.ICGtesting.com
Printed in the USA
LVHW080602130120
643361LV00015BA/991/P